THE HERITAGE BOOK

1979

THE HERITAGE BOOK

1979

Edna McCann

Macmillan Publishing Co., Inc.
New York

Macmillan Publishing Co., Inc.
866 Third Avenue, New York, N.Y. 10022

Library of Congress Cataloging in Publication Data

McCann, Edna.
The heritage book, 1979.

1. Devotional calendars. I. Title.
BV4810.M332 242'.2 77-7141
ISBN 0-02-582910-6

First American Edition 1978

Printed in Canada

INTRODUCTION

When I was a young woman, I began collecting stories, verses, and quotations from my friends and family and pasting them into scrapbooks. Often, when a problem arose, I would search in my books for an appropriate few lines to cheer a friend who was ill or comfort someone who was facing a particular trial. Indeed, I often used the material myself when I needed a fresh perspective on my own life and its quandaries.

During those years my children also sought recourse to "mother's scrapbooks" and it was at their urging many years later that I wrote the first *Heritage Book*. Since the first book I have received letters and messages from people all over the world who often contribute stories from their own lives or send me accounts and verses they think will be useful to me. I often bless the day that my children encouraged me to begin the *Heritage Book* because it has enabled me to make so many new friends and acquaintances. It has also shown me that the human qualities of love and laughter, courage and sympathy, continue to exist despite all dire predictions from the more pessimistic of today's social prophets.

My special prayer for 1979 is that this small book may contribute a measure of those qualities to your life and that you may prosper and be happy with each new day.

E. McC.

Toronto, August 1978

JANUARY

MONDAY—JANUARY 1

As we enter the New Year, let us try to remember what the famous American humorist Mark Twain said near the end of his life: "I am an old man and have known a great many troubles, but most of them never happened." How true that is — most of our worries about the future are so unnecessary. Shall we keep that in mind as we look forward to a happy and prosperous New Year?

TUESDAY — JANUARY 2

We were all surprised to see one of our community's well-known agnostics at church last week. We kind of thought it had something to do with the Christmas season. But my friend Will told me that when he had hinted to the man that this might be the reason, the man replied: "No, Will, I haven't changed my mind, but every so often I like to hear another man who believes what he says, and the only one I can think of is the minister of this church."

WEDNESDAY — JANUARY 3

I like this description of the twelve months of the year by writer George Ellis:

Snowy, Flowy, Blowy,
Showery, Flowery, Bowery,
Hoppy, Droppy, Croppy,
Breezy, Sneezy, Freezy.

Today it is definitely "snowy" and I decided to sit by the fire and read a good book. There are some compensations for a January day, after all.

THURSDAY — JANUARY 4

Patience does not help always; impatience never does.

— *Russian proverb*

FRIDAY — JANUARY 5

THE Lord said, "Let there be wheat," and Saskatchewan was born.

I like that remark by Stephen Leacock. Too often people from Eastern Canada forget how much we owe the farmers on the Prairies. Leacock, the great satirist, no doubt was being cynical, but as an economist he knew what he was talking about.

SATURDAY — JANUARY 6

A young neighbor of mine dropped in yesterday for a cup of tea. Apparently her young daughter had been particularly trying and her husband had turned to his wife and asked, "Do you think we should take our daughter to a psychologist to find out what's wrong with us?"

"How that man makes me laugh," she said, her eyes sparkling. It's probably true that laughter is the cement that holds a marriage together.

SUNDAY — JANUARY 7

BETTER a humble lot, and the fear of the Lord present, than great riches that leave a man unsatisfied.

MONDAY — JANUARY 8

WHEN I asked Dr. G. which disease he found hardest to treat, he paused and replied thoughtfully, "Self-pity."

"But surely that isn't a disease," I said. "It can stop the body from healing, the mind from mending, and if a patient is obsessed by it, a doctor has a difficult time curing any other disease the patient may have," Dr. G. answered.

TUESDAY — JANUARY 9

WHEN I was a little girl, I asked for a pony for my birthday, and I added nightly prayer to daily badgering of my parents. I never got the pony but I did receive something precious. When my minister father finally said, "You're going to have to face it, I can't give you a pony," I replied, "Maybe there will be a miracle."

"There's more to a miracle than getting what you want," my father said. "Sometimes a much greater miracle happens when you don't get it."

I have yet to meet anyone who does not find comfort once that this fact is grasped: There is no unanswered prayer. True, God does not always answer yes, but He does answer.

WEDNESDAY — JANUARY 10

I read recently that probably the most popular medical book ever was a textbook of hygiene written in Latin verse about 1100 A.D.. Translated by the godson of Queen Elizabeth I it was widely used as a home health book; even today some of it is worth remembering:

Joy, Temperance and Repose
Slam the door on the doctor's nose.

<u>THURSDAY — JANUARY 11</u>

A long life may be good enough, but a good life is never long enough.

— *Benjamin Franklin*

<u>FRIDAY — JANUARY 12</u>

WHEN my grandson Fred was recently planning a trip, the children protested leaving the family pet, a lovely cocker spaniel, at home. When Fred wrote the hotel asking if the pet could stay with them in their room, he was surprised to receive this reply:

"I've been in the hotel business thirty years. Never had to call the police to eject a disorderly dog, never had a dog set the bedclothes on fire from smoking, never found a hotel blanket or two in a dog's suitcase. Sure the dog's welcome.

P.S. If he'll vouch for you, come along too."

<u>SATURDAY — JANUARY 13</u>

TALK to a man about himself, and he will listen for hours.

— *Benjamin Disraeli*

SUNDAY — JANUARY 14

GOD at the beginning of time created heaven and earth. Earth was still an empty waste and darkness hung over the deep; but already, over its waters, stirred the breath of God.

MONDAY — JANUARY 15

DON'T flatter yourself that friendship authorizes you to say disagreeable things to your intimates. The nearer you come to a relation with a person, the more necessary do tact and courtesy become.

— *Oliver Wendell Holmes*

TUESDAY — JANUARY 16

MY granddaughter Frances wrote me a letter in which she said she knew her life would be so much happier if she were not shy. I wrote her right back and told her not to worry. Why, the person who isn't shy in his or her teens will be a bore in middle age. Shyness is the protective fluid in which the personality develops. It is a gift, not an affliction in the young and shows a sensitivity which will turn them finally into open and lovable adults.

WEDNESDAY — JANUARY 17

WOULDN'T it be wonderful if we could learn the trick of living more in the present than in the past? This is especially important for us older folk who tend to dwell in the past. Yet the past is gone beyond prayer. There is only one world pressing against us at this minute and in that minute you are alive in the here and now. The best way to live is by accepting each minute as an unrepeatable miracle.

I'm going to try to remember to really live in the present for at least part of each day. Why don't you try, too?

THURSDAY — JANUARY 18

THE feet find the road easy when the heart walks with them.

— *Russian proverb*

FRIDAY — JANUARY 19

"MEDIOCRITY is the easiest thing in the world to achieve," said Erik Bruhn whose own brilliant dancing career proves his own words don't apply to him. But he is so right about many of us: we let ourselves be satisfied with far too little.

SATURDAY — JANUARY 20

PARENTS, I have often observed, tend to treasure and overprotect their best-looking children. What parents of such children should recognize is the extra responsibility they have to see that these children have normal opportunities for personal development.

Avoid the temptation to ride on their outer glory.

SUNDAY — JANUARY 21

YOU must serve God or money; you cannot serve both.

MONDAY — JANUARY 22

CHRISTIE is a friend of my granddaughter Phyllis, and a schoolteacher. Her first-grade children were having a wonderful time playing with a stray cat they had brought into the classroom one day. After a while one little boy asked Christie if it was a boy or a girl. Not wishing to get into that particular subject, Christie said she couldn't tell. "I know how we can find out," said the little boy. "All right," said Christie, resigning herself to the inevitable, "How?" "We can vote," said the child.

TUESDAY — JANUARY 23

I have known couples who are so rigidly conventional that they don't even get any fun out of their so-called amusements. They play golf or bridge not because they enjoy these activities, but because it's the thing to do.

What on earth can such people bring to the lives of their families and children?

WEDNESDAY — JANUARY 24

TOO often people believe that nothing is easier than to love. The truth is very much another matter. While every human being has a capacity for love, its realization requires time and energy and work.

We should treasure those who have learned how to love.

THURSDAY — JANUARY 25

TODAY is the birthday of the poet Robert Burns. I've always been fond of his *Selkirk Grace*:

Some hae meat, and canna eat,
   And some wad eat that want it;
But we hae meat, and we can eat,
   And sae the Lord be thankit.

FRIDAY — JANUARY 26

I found this little story in the church newspaper yesterday. Reverend Browne was asked by a parishioner why the local ministers were seen gathering at his house every Monday morning. "To tell the truth," said Reverend Browne, "we exchange sermons." "Well don't do it!" warned the lady, "you get stuck every time."

SATURDAY — JANUARY 27

MY son-in-law Bruce who is teaching English to young immigrants at night school, showed me this poem by one of the students, who was confused by the English language.

The wind was rough,
And cold and blough;
She kept her hands inside her mough;
It chilled her through,
Her nose turned blough,
And still the squall the faster flough.

SUNDAY — JANUARY 28

EVERY idle word men shall speak, they shall give account thereof on the day of judgment.

MONDAY — JANUARY 29

TODAY the hungry peoples of the world are knocking at our door. If we do not answer, they may hammer it down.

— *Paul Martin, former Canadian external affairs minister*

TUESDAY — JANUARY 30

MY granddaughter Phyllis dropped in last night after her exercise class. She said it was packed with women who had gained too much weight during Christmas and were trying to lose it before their holiday trips south. "Not enough hard work," I grumped, "that's all that's the matter with them."

But it does seem that something's wrong when half the world is dieting and the other half goes to bed hungry.

WEDNESDAY — JANUARY 31

IN order to maintain a balanced perspective on life, the person who has a dog to worship him should also have a cat to ignore him.

— *Peterborough Examiner*

FEBRUARY

THURSDAY — FEBRUARY 1

"**J**UST when is the right time to end a visit to someone's home?" asked the young newlywed from down the street. So we both put our heads together and came up with these suggestions:

A dinner party — about one hour after coffee is served.

A luncheon — 30 or 40 minutes after dessert.

An afternoon call — no longer than an hour.

A cocktail party — about an hour and a half.

I hope this bit of guidance will be helpful, although I never attend cocktail parties.

FRIDAY — FEBRUARY 2

I often tell parents of anxious teenagers that a boy (or girl) becomes an adult three years *before* his parents think he has — and about two years *after* he thinks he has.

Once parents are aware of this secret, they seem to have fewer troubles with adolescents.

SATURDAY — FEBRUARY 3

EDUCATION is turning things over in **the** mind.

— Robert Frost

SUNDAY — FEBRUARY 4

WHENCE then cometh wisdom? And where is the place of understanding?

Seeing is hid from the eyes of all living, and kept close from the fowls of the air.

MONDAY — FEBRUARY 5

ARCHIBALD Lampman, the nineteenth-century poet, has some wise words and some sad ones too about our severe winters:

Winter for reading and study; summer for loafing and dreaming and getting close to nature; spring and autumn for joyous production. The mind does not mount readily to the higher exertions during the severity of our winter season.

If we can just hold on a little longer, we will soon be reacquainted with the pleasures of spring. Like all my friends, I can hardly wait.

TUESDAY — FEBRUARY 6

WORRY never robs tomorrow of its sorrow, it only robs today of its strength.

— *A. J. Cronin*

WEDNESDAY — FEBRUARY 7

I think it's wonderful to see my great-grand-children so concerned about the treatment of animals and scornful of any woman who wears a fur coat made from the skins of animals in danger of extinction. But like every new generation, they think they were the first to feel outrage about cruelty towards our little friends.

I quote these lines from William Blake to show that this great poet as far back as the eighteenth century, also cared:

> *A dog starv'd at this master's gate*
> *Predicts the ruin of the State,*
> *A horse misused upon the road*
> *Calls to Heaven for human blood.*
> *Each outcry of the hunted hare*
> *A fiber from the brain does tear,*
> *A skylark wounded in the wing,*
> *A cherubim does cease to sing.*

THURSDAY — FEBRUARY 8

HAPPINESS is the only thing we can give without having.

FRIDAY — FEBRUARY 9

I saw this pinned up in the window of my friend Jake Frampton who owns a bookstore:

On his 90th birthday, the American critic Louis Untermeyer said, "I'm writing my third autobiography . . . the other two were premature."

SATURDAY — FEBRUARY 10

OLD Mr. Meers never drove an automobile but he certainly taught one young man a powerful lesson.

While crossing King Street, Mr. Meers was nearly hit by an impatient young driver who said, "Relax, Pop, I missed you, didn't I?"

Angrily Mr. Meers approached the car, lifted his heavy cane, and swung it just near enough to the driver's head to make him cry out, "Hey, take it easy."

"Now, *you* just relax, son," said Mr. Meers, "I missed you, didn't I?"

That young man will never take old people for granted again.

SUNDAY — FEBRUARY 11

REMEMBER that thou magnify his work, which men behold.

Every man may see it; man may behold it afar off.

Behold, God is great, and we know him not, neither can the number of his years be searched out.

For he maketh small the drops of water: they pour down rain according to the vapor thereof.

Which the clouds do drop and distil upon man abundantly.

MONDAY — FEBRUARY 12

"WE have really learned to pray," said Hattie this afternoon, "when we realize that praying is a privilege rather than a duty."

TUESDAY — FEBRUARY 13

WHAT we are is God's gift to us.
What we become is our gift to God.
— *Louis Nizer*

WEDNESDAY — FEBRUARY 14

PERHAPS it's a bit of a jolt to present this Eskimo proverb on St. Valentine's Day; but a shock is good for us every now and again.

Love comes after marriage.

Ada Crombie told me that, and she firmly believes it. And her own happy marriage, now in its forty-seventh year, seems to prove her point.

THURSDAY — FEBRUARY 15

TO love a person implies caring for and feeling responsible for his life, for the growth and development of all his human powers.

— *Erich Fromm*

FRIDAY — FEBRUARY 16

OLD? I am not old. Let me see . . . seven and five . . . that is twelve. Yes, I am twelve years old . . . you might say.

Tired? One is never tired in the service of the Master.

— *Brother André at seventy-five*

SATURDAY — FEBRUARY 17

TOO often these days you hear about computer dating services and see slightly suggestive advertisements even in our daily newspapers. So I was glad when a friend on holiday in Arizona sent me this down-to-earth advertisement, which she claims is true:

Farmer, aged 36, wishes to meet woman around 30 who owns a tractor. Enclosed photo of tractor.

SUNDAY — FEBRUARY 18

THEREFORE God give thee of the dew of heaven, and the fatness of the earth, and plenty of corn and wine.

MONDAY — FEBRUARY 19

FROM a physical point of view a vacation in January or February is more necessary when you live in Canada than holidays in summer. If even more people were aware of this simple truth, and I am glad to see that many are, there would be far fewer illnesses during these cold winter months.

TUESDAY — FEBRUARY 20

IN the presence of trouble some people grow wings; others buy crutches.

WEDNESDAY — FEBRUARY 21

"WHAT next!" exclaimed my grandson Marshall, reading the paper last evening. The government now has some big muckamuck who's sole job is to look after supplies of paper. What's this country coming to?"

I can't altogether approve of Marshall's anger, but it is reassuring that our young people, even in these extravagant times, value the old-fashioned virtues of thrift and economy.

THURSDAY — FEBRUARY 22

MY cousin Wilma, once volunteered to work as a nurse's aide in a hospital in London, Ontario, where she lived. One morning, as she began to bathe one of her patients the woman put out a hand to stop her. "Did you once have a small boy in your family?" she asked. "Why, yes," Wilma said, puzzled. "I thought so," the patient said, "That's exactly the way you're washing my face."

FRIDAY — FEBRUARY 23

THE beaver is a great symbol for Canada. He's so busy chewing, he can't see what's going on.

— Barry Mason

In these troubled times, I fear that remark is all too often true.

SATURDAY — FEBRUARY 24

MEN must be governed by God, or they will be ruled by tyrants.

— William Penn

Think but a moment of all the dictators in the world. These men — along with their subjects — unfortunately no longer have respect for religious or moral values.

SUNDAY — FEBRUARY 25

AND he said unto his disciples, Therefore I say unto you, Take no thought for your life, what ye shall eat; neither for the body, what ye shall put on.

The life is more than meat, and the body is more than raiment.

MONDAY — FEBRUARY 26

IN my many years of living, I can't very often tell which experience was a knock and which was a boost. But it sure has been interesting, and will continue to be so.

TUESDAY — FEBRUARY 27

AFTER moving from a tiny office into a more spacious one at the University of Toronto, Sir Frederick Banting, the co-discoverer of insulin, is said to have remarked to a friend: "The one thing I dread is affluence. I have a lovely office now, with pictures on the wall and a swivel chair, and I can't do anything."

It's nice to know that Dr. Banting never forgot how constricting power and affluence really are. None of us can afford to forget this lesson.

WEDNESDAY — FEBRUARY 28

A religion that is small enough for our understanding would not be large enough for our needs.

— *Arthur Balfour*

MARCH

THURSDAY — MARCH 1

JAKE and I were musing in his bookstore the other morning. "You know," he said, "as each of us grows older we should carefully examine our own personalities, because what exists today will still be there tomorrow but magnified many, many times. If at thirty someone is self-centred, well, that same someone will just get worse as the years go by." Then he laughed, "Can you imagine what they'd be like at our age?"

FRIDAY — MARCH 2

MY nice young neighbor down the street held a birthday party for her eight-year-old this week. We all volunteered to help keep the party going and rushed around organizing games, treasure hunts, and races. In the midst of this my neighbor's son turned to his mother and asked, "When this is all over, can we play?" He really brought us all up short. We had forgotten that children like to play their games privately.

SATURDAY — MARCH 3

I have never told this story before, but now I think is the time. On the eve of my wedding, my grandmother took me aside and gave me this advice: "Remember, try to find some way to stay happy. When you're sad, you'll look plain; when you look plain, you'll grow bitter; when you are bitter, you'll be disagreeable; and a disagreeable person can never be happy."

I was not always successful, but I think George would have agreed that we were very often happy.

SUNDAY — MARCH 4

BE sure you do not perform your acts of piety before men for them to watch; if you do that, you have no title to a reward from your Father who is in heaven.

MONDAY — MARCH 5

THE sublime and the ridiculous are often so nearly related that it is difficult to class them separately. One step above the sublime makes the ridiculous, and one step above the ridiculous makes the sublime again.

— *Thomas Paine*

TUESDAY — MARCH 6

BECAUSE of a local postal dispute I did not get any mail yesterday. How I miss letters from my friends! Coincidentally, I came across these remarks about Sir William Mulock who was Canadian postmaster-general at the turn of the century.

The tribute first appeared in a Montreal newspaper.

> *The post office department has been a changed institution since the day he took charge of it.*
>
> *He found it honeycombed with abuses, abuses that cost the country hundreds of thousands of dollars annually and served no more useful purpose than the gratification of a partisan worker, here and there.*
>
> *By dint of painstaking application, making every move tell, he has been able to considerably reduce the normal deficit and at the same time lower the rate of postage in Canada.*

WEDNESDAY — MARCH 7

JAKE Frampton is a great fan of the American poet Robert Frost. Here's a short poem of his that Jake knew I would like:

> *If one by one we counted people out*
> *For the least sin, it wouldn't take us long*
> *To get so we had no one left to live with;*
> *For to be social is to be forgiving.*

THURSDAY — MARCH 8

THE best reason for holding your chin up when in trouble is that it keeps the mouth closed.

FRIDAY — MARCH 9

WHEN I hear young women complain about housework these days, I think of my friend Laura's grandmother who homesteaded on the Prairies. She worked an eighteen-hour day, made all her own bread, butter, preserves, and soap, had an acre of vegetable garden, sewed all her children's clothes (there were seven of them), and lived to be ninety.

She told me once, "Only thing makes me anxious is sitting. I don't seem to know how to do it."

SATURDAY—MARCH 10

I found a photograph yesterday of my brother as a boy standing beside a wall he had helped my father build. Ben had complained about the length of time the job was taking because my father, who had learned the craft from *his* father was being so thorough and slow.

My father was very particular that each rock be chinked, even those in the foundation trench below the surface. Finally, my brother blurted out, "But who's going to know if those rocks are chinked or not?" My father's astonishment was genuine, as he peered over his spectacles. "Why," he said, "I will — and so will you."

SUNDAY — MARCH 11

LORD, thou has been our dwelling place in all generations.

Before the mountains were brought forth,

Or ever thou hadst formed the earth and the world,

Even from everlasting to everlasting, thou art God.

MONDAY — MARCH 12

DON'T be troubled if the temptation to give advice is irresistible; the ability to ignore it is universal.

TUESDAY — MARCH 13

A few hours before the last snowstorm my friend Muriel and I went downtown to shop and took the subway part way home. We got on the bus inside the station and were totally unprepared to find the street blanketed with snow when we wanted to get off.

But we did have a laugh when the bus conductor called out, "All gentlemen with big feet get off first and make tracks for the ladies." I guess chivalry isn't dead after all.

WEDNESDAY — MARCH 14

MY neighbor told me that her husband during a conversation with their son stated, "The trouble with you is you're always wishing for things you don't have." "But Dad, what else are you supposed to wish for?" countered the youngster.

THURSDAY — MARCH 15

THE heights by great men reached and kept
    were not attained by sudden flight,
But they, while their companions slept,
Were toiling upward in the night.
               — *Henry Wadsworth Longfellow*

FRIDAY — MARCH 16

FRIENDS of mine took their six-year-old daughter Karen to the new Metro Zoo in Toronto. They had a wonderful time wandering around and finally arrived at the polar bears. For the longest time, Karen studied the bears, and finally turned to her mother and said, "I sure would like to see them eat somebody."

SATURDAY — MARCH 17

TODAY is St. Patrick's Day, and a friend in northeastern Quebec sent me a recipe which traveled from Ireland to that part of Canada. The name of the dish is Colcannon, and it's simply potatoes and turnips pounded together and fried in butter. My friend told me that in her region of Quebec it's traditional to serve this Irish dish on Colcannon Night, which is our Hallowe'en.

SUNDAY — MARCH 18

AMONG you the greatest of all is to be the servant of all; the man who exalts himself will be humbled and the man who humbles himself will be exalted.

MONDAY — MARCH 19

MY friend Emily from Philadelphia wrote me a letter and said she had been feeling a bit down so she decided to get busy and clean out her dresser drawers. In one of them she found a photograph of her grandmother. Left a widow at the age of thirty by the accidental death of her husband, she had set to work and with incredible perserverance and self-sacrifice, had educated her boys through college and seen them all rise to positions of importance.

Emily wrote that when she once asked her grandmother how she had accomplished this, she said simply, "I was never one to sit down and feel sorry for myself." Emily said she was glad she found the photograph because it changed her whole day and lifted her spirits.

TUESDAY — MARCH 20

AFTER the wedding of my youngest daughter Mary I broke down and cried. I felt utterly isolated. For twenty-five years my children had absorbed so much of my time and thoughts. While I was feeling sorry for myself, my husband George came into the room.

"What am I going to do?" I moaned. "All the children have gone."

George waited a moment and then said very quietly, "You might remember you're married to me."

For years I have been grateful to George for that remark. Before our daughter's wedding we had a good life together; *afterwards* it was wonderful.

WEDNESDAY — MARCH 21

I read this in the newspaper the other day, and it so amused me I would like to pass it on.

When a local truck driver was asked to explain a collision to the police, he answered, "I was backing out of Frederick's Body Shop, and by the time I backed out far enough to see what was coming, it already had."

THURSDAY — MARCH 22

BRUCE, my son-in-law, is having such a good time teaching young immigrants English at night school. He recently asked them to write a brief letter in English that some well-known man might have written during his lifetime.

Bruce was hardly prepared for one student's brief note:

"Dear Josephine,

I am sorry to inform you that I didn't make out very well in Waterloo.

Love,

Napoleon."

FRIDAY — MARCH 23

ALTHOUGH spring is now officially here, it never seems to really come to Canada until well into April. That's why I like this verse sent to me by a friend in the Maritimes.

Though poets have told us brightly
That spring on dancing feet comes lightly,
It seems to be, she really sloshes
Along in roomy old galoshes.

SATURDAY — MARCH 24

OLD Mrs. Borgstrum has been a semi-recluse for years. She now seems to have made an important medical discovery.

Every morning she goes to a nearby laundromat and sits with her back against the extractor. She claims the old machine, which gives off a great deal of heat does wonders for her back. Mrs. Borgstrum chats with her neighbors for forty minutes or so and then goes off home.

My granddaughter Phyllis insists that the cure is simpler still; at last, old Mrs. Borgstrum has some company.

SUNDAY — MARCH 25

O clap your hands, all ye people, shout unto God with the voice of triumph.

For the Lord most high, is terrible; he is a great King over all the earth.

He shall subdue the people under us, and the nations under our feet.

He shall choose our inheritance for us, the excellency of Jacob whom he loved.

MONDAY — MARCH 26

THESE words of wisdom by Oliver Wendell Holmes struck me as something my granddaughter Frances might appreciate. She sometimes worries too much about being different from her schoolmates.

"The longer I live, the more satisfied I am of two things: first, that the truest lives are those that are cut rose-diamond fashion, with many facets answering to the many-planed aspects of the world about them; secondly, that society is always trying in some way or other to grind us down to a single flat surface. It is hard work to resist the grinding-down action."

TUESDAY — MARCH 27

MORALE is when your hands and feet keep working although your head says it can't be done.

WEDNESDAY — MARCH 28

THE trees to their innermost marrow are touched by the sun;
The robin is here and the sparrow; Spring is begun!

— *Archibald Lampman*

THURSDAY — MARCH 29

"SPRING has come and the chirds are birping." Some radio announcer made that blooper long ago, and I have never forgotten it. Poor man, he was so excited to see the last of the snow and feel the warmth of the sun. He would have done better to remember these lines from the seventeenth-century poet, John Dowland:

> *Look how the snowy mountains*
> *Heaven's sun doth gently waste.*

FRIDAY — MARCH 30

FROM a country doctor some advice that we should all heed:

Do I maintain an unrelenting pace, or have I learned the value of setting aside some time each day for mental and physical relaxation?

To the second part of the question I pray we can all answer Yes.

SATURDAY — MARCH 31

THE trouble with some self-made men is that they insist on giving everybody their recipe.

APRIL

SUNDAY — APRIL 1

SANCTIFY ye a fast, call a solemn assembly, gather the elders and all the inhabitants of the land into the house of the Lord your God, and cry unto the Lord.

MONDAY — APRIL 2

WELL, yesterday was April Fools' Day, but nothing untoward happened to me. So in honor of the day, I will just record this observation by Mark Twain:

Good breeding consists in concealing how much we think of ourselves — and how little we think of the other person.

The remark is a bit uncharitable, but it reminds me of a man just like the one Twain describes.

TUESDAY — APRIL 3

CANADA has never been a melting pot — more like a tossed salad.

— *Arnold Edinborough*

WEDNESDAY — APRIL 4

HERE'S a story I hadn't heard before about my personal hero, Sir Winston Churchill, sent along to me by a reader in St. Catharines, Ontario.

In the early days of the war, Churchill motored hurriedly to Canterbury to see that proper precautions were being taken for the protection of the famous cathedral there. Later he explained to the Archbishop, "We have applied every possible protective device we can. No matter how many close hits the Nazis make, I feel sure the cathedral will survive."

"Ah yes, close hits," said the Archbishop gloomily, "but what if they score a direct hit upon us?"

"In that case," decided Churchill, "you will have to regard it, my dear Archbishop, as a summons."

THURSDAY — APRIL 5

ON her birthday my granddaughter Joanne received this short note from her husband: "To Joanne, my wife, with whom it's as easy to keep in love as to fall in love."

I was so touched by their happiness.

FRIDAY — APRIL 6

A few months ago my friend Jim retired as foreman of a furniture plant because he had reached the age of sixty-five. Now he and his brother-in-law have opened a carpenter's shop. And very handsome it is, too.

"We were both bored," Jim explained to me, "and now we're working harder and better than ever. You know, we had to prove to ourselves, as well as to others, that we were not old and useless." It seems to me they've already proved it!

SATURDAY — APRIL 7

THERE'S so much love and tenderness in this verse:
Warm summer sun, shine kindly here;
Warm southern wind, blow softly here;
Green sod above lie light, lie light,
Good night, dear heart, good night,
good night.

That prayer was found inscribed on the tombstone of Olivia Susan Clemens, Mark Twain's daughter. I like to think her father wrote these words for her.

SUNDAY—APRIL 8

CHARITY never faileth: but whether there be prophecies they shall fall; whether there be tongues, they shall cease; whether there be knowledge, it shall vanish away.

For we know in part, and we prophesy in part.

But when that which is perfect is come, then that which is in part shall be done away.

When I was a child, I spake as a child, I understood as a child, I thought as a child: but when I became a man, I put away childish things.

For now we see through a glass, darkly; but then face to face: now I know in part; but then shall I know even as also I am known.

And now abideth faith, hope, charity, these **three**; but the greatest of these is charity.

MONDAY — APRIL 9

THE measure of a man's real character is what he would do if he knew he would never be found out.

— *Thomas Babington Macaulay*

Need I add that the remark is true for **women, too**?

TUESDAY — APRIL 10

MY granddaughter Phyllis has become very interested in the rights of the elderly.

The other day she was addressing a local meeting, and made a telling comparison between the young and the old. First she praised the freshness and openness of youth — their beauty. Then she went on to say, with a lovely smile of her own, "but beautiful young people are accidents of nature; beautiful old people are works of art."

She was warmly applauded, and I felt very proud.

WEDNESDAY — APRIL 11

THE only gift is a portion of thyself.
— *Ralph Waldo Emerson*

THURSDAY — APRIL 12

"THE hand that rocks the cradle does not rule the world." So said that passionate suffragette Nellie McClung many years ago. She went on to prove her point: "If it did, human life would be held dearer and the world would be a sweeter, cleaner, safer place than it is now."

FRIDAY — APRIL 13

AND they took Jesus, and led him away.

And he bearing his cross went forth into a place called the place of a skull, which is called in the Hebrew Golgotha: Where they crucified him, and two others with him, on either side one, and Jesus in the midst.

And Pilate wrote a title, and put it on the cross. And the writing was, JESUS OF NAZARETH THE KING OF THE JEWS.

This title then read many of the Jews; for the place where Jesus was crucified was nigh to the city: and it was written in Hebrew, and Greek, and Latin.

Then said the chief priests of the Jews to Pilate, Write not, The King of the Jews: but that he said, I am King of the Jews.

Pilate answered, What I have written I have written.

SATURDAY — APRIL 14

SWALLOWS must be the best-loved birds in the western world. Although owls, ravens, and eagles are considered birds of ill omen in folklore, the swallow brings glad tidings of comfort and joy. According to Christian legend, it was a swallow who tried to console Christ while He was on the cross.

SUNDAY — APRIL 15

NOW upon the first day of the week, **very** early in the morning, they came unto **the** sepulchre, bringing the spices which they had prepared, and certain others with them.

And they found the stone rolled away from the sepulchre.

And they entered in, and found not the body of the Lord Jesus.

And it came to pass, as they were much perplexed thereabout, behold, two men stood by them in shining garments: And as they were afraid, and bowed down their faces to the earth, they said unto them, Why seek ye the living among the dead?

He is not here, but is risen: remember how he spake unto you when he was yet in Galilee,

Saying, The Son of man must be delivered into the hands of sinful men, and be crucified, and the third day rise again.

And they remembered his words,

And returned from the sepulchre, and told all these things unto the eleven, and to all the rest.

HE IS RISEN, THE LORD IS RISEN INDEED.

MONDAY — APRIL 16

ON a quiet day, with no shopping or visiting to do, I like to reflect on my life and values. For example, do I merely pay lip service to my religious beliefs, or are they a practical, dynamic part of my daily life?

I offer that question to my readers in the hope that while reflecting upon it, they will discover the same satisfaction I have.

TUESDAY — APRIL 17

HERE'S a lovely thought I came across in a book called *The Treasure of the Humble*: "Friends and lovers do not know each other until they can be silent together."

WEDNESDAY — APRIL 18

"NOTHING more is needed for the walker's pleasure," recorded Ralph Waldo Emerson, "than endurance, plain clothes, old shoes, an eye for nature, good humor, vast curiosity, good speech, (and) good silence."

St. Francis of Assisi delighted in walking through the Umbrian Hills, singing praises to God, of the beauty of the hills, trees, wild flowers, and birds.

THURSDAY — APRIL 19

THERE are touches of spring everywhere. I usually spend a few days at Eastertime with my good friends Joan and Jim. Yesterday Joan and I went for an afternoon walk in a fine rain.

We agreed that a spring walk in the rain refreshes a person as much as the spring rain does the grass. And the sparrows chirped more sweetly than I can ever remember.

FRIDAY — APRIL 20

A man will sometimes devote his whole life to the development of one part of his body — his wishbone.

SATURDAY — APRIL 21

SOME in their discourse desire rather commendation of wit in being able to hold all arguments, than of judgment in discerning what is true, as if it were a praise to know what might be said, and not what should be **thought**.

— Francis Bacon

SUNDAY — APRIL 22

BRETHREN, if a man be overtaken in a fault, ye which are spiritual, restore such a one in the spirit of meekness; considering thyself, lest thou also be tempted.

Bear ye one another's burdens, and so fulfil the law of Christ.

For if a man think himself to be something, when he is nothing, he deceiveth himself.

But let every man prove his own work, and then shall he have rejoicing in himself alone, and not in another.

For every man shall bear his own burden.

MONDAY —APRIL 23

"HAVING a wonderful time. Wish you were here."

Nancy O'Brien received that postcard message from her husband today, and was furious. He seemed to be saying that being without her was wonderful.

I suggested to Nancy that she had misread Bill's message. What he really wanted was her there to share with him a lovely experience.

Postcards should be large enough to contain what we really want to say.

TUESDAY — APRIL 24

MY son-in-law John announced at dinner last night that a stiff dose of taxes might help the country get over inflation.

"It would certainly force us to learn to live within our means," said one of the guests.

A young student sitting near me quietly said, "High taxes are no more a cure for inflation than alcohol is for a diseased liver."

We were all appropriately chastened.

WEDNESDAY — APRIL 25

HE who does not speak is not heard by God.
— *Indian saying*

THURSDAY — APRIL 26

IF ever Confederation fails, it will not be because Quebec — the political voice of French Canada — has separated from it. It will be because the way to keep Quebec in has not been found.

These thoughts of Jean Lesage, a former premier of Quebec, are worth considering and talking about. Every Canadian, English or French-speaking, should be doing as much.

FRIDAY — APRIL 27

WHENEVER we feel tempted to pity ourselves here's a list of indomitable people we should remember: Helen Keller, who became one of the foremost citizens of her day despite incredible afflictions; Robert Louis Stevenson, who produced masterpieces of literature although he suffered from tuberculosis; Father Damien continued his wonderful work among the lepers although he himself was dying of the disease. Countless unknown, ordinary people have overcome illness, hardship, and pain and have lived cheerful and successful lives. Consider them and then, if you dare, be sorry for yourself.

SATURDAY—APRIL 28

I just had a letter from my childhood friend Mavis Turnridge in which she related an amusing incident that recently happened to her. She was leaving church when a dear old lady came up to her and asked, "Is your name Mary Anne Varley?" "No, it isn't," Mavis replied. "Thank goodness," the old lady said, "If it was, I was going to have to tell you you've changed an awful lot."

SUNDAY — APRIL 29

FOR God shall bring every work into judgment, with every secret thing, whether it be good, or whether it be evil.

MONDAY — APRIL 30

MANY years ago, when Dr. G. (now a distinguished specialist) was a young medical student he became very discouraged because he found that some patients were so exasperated after all the doctors had questioned them endlessly, that when *he* got to them they were reluctant to give him the information he needed. In despair, he complained to an older doctor on the staff. "Why it's very simple," the wise doctor told him, "Just ask them how they've been sleeping. Everyone loves to talk about their sleeping habits. Once you've got them interested, they'll tell you everything else you need to know." And the young medical student discovered it worked.

"Still use that trick even today," Dr. G. confided to me. Seems it's true — sleep is important to just about everyone. Just try asking your friends how they are sleeping these days.

MAY

TUESDAY — MAY 1

MY granddaughter Phyllis came over yesterday afternoon to ask me to start collecting empty tin cans now. In December her class will make Christmas tree ornaments from them and present them as gifts to the local school committee and to hospital groups.

I sat right down and wrote to my friend Peggy Johnson in England about it. In letters Peggy is always complaining that the younger generation is so wasteful and careless. I told Peggy that I could see a real attempt on the part of today's youngsters to make do with whatever's at hand.

WEDNESDAY — MAY 2

WHEN someone asked the Harveys the secret of a happy marriage on their golden wedding anniversary this week, Mrs. Harvey replied, "Well, it helped a lot to know at the start that the path of true love didn't lead over to my mother's house when things got difficult."

THURSDAY — MAY 3

ON television last night they interviewed young men from Cape Breton Island who are unemployed and find it hard to get work in the economically depressed area. But none of them wanted to leave the Maritimes to find work elsewhere where jobs might be available. "My family and friends are here," one young man explained. "We stick together; when times are hard, we help each other out. And," he added, "people here smile more than they do elsewhere." Seems to me good and sound reasons to stay. What do you think?

FRIDAY — MAY 4

DO what you can, with what you have, where you are.

— *Theodore Roosevelt*

SATURDAY — MAY 5

WHEN I asked our neighborhood's leading gardener Will Hampton to explain how he grows the most beautiful flowers for miles around, he just laughed and said his green thumb came from the mistakes he had made while learning to see things from the plant's point of view.

SUNDAY — MAY 6

HOW plain are the duties that which the Lord enjoins, the treasure of man's heart; how clear is the commandment the Lord gives, the enlightenment of man's eyes.

MONDAY — MAY 7

MY granddaughter Phyllis told me about a new young teacher at her school who came into the office looking harassed. "He asked me for one of the IQ forms," Phyllis told me, "and when I asked him what he was going to do with just one test, he replied, 'Oh, I just want to find out if it's them or *me*.'"

TUESDAY—MAY 8

MY friend Maureen McKenna in Alberta sent me this amusing verse about this month:

May be chill, may be mild,
May pour, may snow,
May be still, may be wild,
May lower, may glow,
May freeze, may burn,
May be gold, may be gray,
May do all these in turn.

WEDNESDAY—MAY 9

BROWSING in our public library one morning I found a quote by Robert Louis Stevenson which startled me, "Extreme busyness, whether at school or college, kirk or market, is a symptom of deficient vitality." Surely he's made a mistake, I thought, and meant "abundant" instead of "deficient." So I read on, "It is no good speaking to such folk; they cannot be idle, their nature is not generous enough."

When I mentioned the quote, which still bothered me, to my friend Will, he said, "Stevenson's right. A lot of people keep so busy getting things done that they reach the end of their lives without ever having lived at all." I think that's worth remembering, for those of us who get so caught up in the daily grind, don't you?

THURSDAY — MAY 10

IN a book called *The Story of Painting*, I read this lovely anecdote about the painter Renoir. Apparently, shortly before his death he painted a watercolor of a bowl of anemones which he said "was his calling card to introduce him to the great painters in heaven."

FRIDAY — MAY 11

I have two close friends, Mary and Gerald Harding, who just retired to a farmhouse in the mountains of British Columbia. They decided to add a terrace to the house to better enjoy the beautiful view, and ordered cement from a neighbor. Taking his time about it, he didn't bring up the first truckload until late one afternoon a few days later.

"Can't you bring one more load today?" Mary pleaded, "we want to get started."

"No, ma'am," the man replied, "Tomorrow will be another day, and if it isn't you won't **need it.**"

SATURDAY — MAY 12

"IF I had my way," a wise old lawyer told me recently, "I'd change the marriage promise to love, honor, and forgive. It would be a healthy reminder of the power that could save many marriages. I've seen men and women just wreck their lives by their inability to forgive one another. Without forgiveness, you lose the power to love. And without love, life has no meaning."

That lawyer was so right — forgiveness is truly the saving grace in our lives.

SUNDAY — MAY 13

I think this poem is a lovely tribute to mothers on their special day.

The golden brooch my mother wore
She left behind for me to wear;
I have no thing I treasure more:
Yet, it is something I could spare.

For if instead she'd left to me
The thing she took into the grave! —
That courage like a rock, which she
Has no more need of, and I have.
—Edna St. Vincent Millay

MONDAY — MAY 14

ONE morning recently I stopped in to see a young married woman who has just moved into our street. "Come into the kitchen while I bathe the baby," she said. Well, the kitchen was a mess — bathinette in the middle of the floor, unwashed dishes in the sink, bottles, formula, squeezed oranges littering the counter. But the baby was adorable. Above the sink was a Phi Beta Kappa key. Marie grinned when she saw me looking at it. "I keep it there to remind me that if I was smart enough to get that, I'm smart enough to get myself out of this mess," she said.

TUESDAY — MAY 15

THE reason that the Ten Commandments are short and clear is that they were handed down direct, not through several committees.

— *John T. Dennis*

WEDNESDAY — MAY 16

MY cousin Lucy was here for a short visit and we were reminiscing about our past and our children.

She told me a story about her daughter Jeannie who, when she was only five years old, got into the habit of rising each morning early and puttering around just long enough to wake the family, only to climb back into bed again. Her reason was always the same — she had to see if there were any surprises. Finally, Lucy told her firmly to stop as there wouldn't be any surprises until Christmas, which was months away.

"I don't mean those kinds of surprises," Jeannie said through her tears. "I mean like yesterday morning it was raining and this morning real summer's here, and tomorrow I'll probably find some pink in the rosebuds." Jeannie still gets up at 5:30 each morning, Lucy told me.

THURSDAY — MAY 17

"YOU know," said my neighbor Dorothy from Number 73, "we should bring back Prohibition."

"It will never work," I said, "though greater control of liquor is a good idea."

"I wasn't thinking of liquor, I was thinking of the word Prohibition," she explained. "Yesterday I read something about a man who in 1904 proclaimed himself a Prohibitionist and then went on to explain what he meant by the word: 'What I propose to prohibit is the reckless use of water.' Good idea, don't you think?"

FRIDAY — MAY 18

JAKE dropped in yesterday to say goodbye for a few weeks. He's off to visit Europe and is very excited about his trip. "You'll have a wonderful time touring," I said. "I'm not touring, I'm traveling," Jake grumped. "There's a big difference between tourists and travelers. Tourists see sights and miss the country. Travelers see the country and the sights too." I wished "the traveler" Godspeed on his "travels."

SATURDAY — MAY 19

WHILE visiting a neighbor this week, her four-year-old daughter frequently came into the house and insisted that her mother "come outside and see." She would then show her mother a flower, a butterfly, a bird's egg, or an ant.

After about the sixth trip, I remarked on my neighbor's patience. "Well," she remarked cheerfully, "I brought her into this world. The least I can do is let her show it to me."

SUNDAY — MAY 20

IF anyone deludes himself he is serving God when he has not learned to control his tongue, must realize that the service he gives is in vain.

MONDAY — MAY 21

TODAY is Victoria Day, a Canadian public holiday. Doug Browne showed me a letter from the Canadian Legion, inviting him to be one of their speakers at the celebration. It read: "The program will include an address by the mayor, a recitation by a high school student, your speech, and then the firing squad."

TUESDAY — MAY 22

I suppose there are few women who reach middle age without beginning to worry about wrinkles and aging. They should remember what the Viennese musical comedy star Lotte Lenya said at age 66 when she was asked if she approved of face lifts. "For myself," the actress said, "maybe ten years from now. I worked hard to get these wrinkles, I want to keep them for a while." Another famous actress, Gloria Swanson, had another philosophy about aging. She said, the real solution was "to fill up your wrinkles with intelligence."

WEDNESDAY — MAY 23

THE other day Muriel and Will invited me to a small restaurant for some oyster stew. When we got there, the owner asked us how hot we liked it. "How hot can you get it?" Will asked. "Well," said the owner, "I can heat it so you can eat it, or I can heat it so you can visit it awhile." So we decided to "visit" it awhile.

THE HERITAGE BOOK

THURSDAY — MAY 24

SOMETIMES I think modern efficiency takes all the flavor out of things. When I was a youngster, we chanted this verse on Queen Victoria's Birthday.

The 24th of May
Is the Queen's Birthday.
If we don't get a holiday,
We'll all run away.

Now Victoria Day is celebrated in Canada on the third Monday in May. But nobody sings that song anymore. But I still do — to myself — every 24th of May.

FRIDAY — MAY 25

HERE'S a charming story I clipped out of the church bulletin.

One night a minister dreamed he saw a new shop in town. He went in and saw an angel behind the counter. Nervously he asked what they sold. "Everything your heart desires," the angel said. "Then I want peace on earth," cried the minister, "an end to sorrow, famine, disease . . ."

"Just one moment," smiled the angel, "You haven't quite understood. We don't sell fruits here, only seeds."

SATURDAY — MAY 26

ONE day this week it rained all morning. It only cleared up after lunch. I was putting away the dishes when I looked out of the window and saw a glorious rainbow in the sky, the first this year.

I was so excited and tried to remember Wordsworth's poem about rainbows. As I don't know it by heart, I went straight to the bookcase and found it.

> My heart leaps up when I behold
>   A rainbow in the sky:
> So was it when my life began;
> So is it now I am a man;
> So be it when I shall grow old,
>   Or let me die!
>
> The Child is father of the Man;
> And I could wish my days to be
> Bound each to each by natural piety.

SUNDAY — MAY 27

AND He said to his disciples, It is impossible that hurt should never be done to men's consciences, but woe betide the man who is the cause of it.

MONDAY — MAY 28

LEST anyone forget during this busy month of May let me remind my American readers that today is Memorial Day, a day on which to remember all those who died for their country.

"Ask not what your country can do for you; ask what you can do for your country."

— John F. Kennedy

TUESDAY — MAY 29

THE Chinese employ ideograms or characters to convey words in their written languages. The character which stands for "good" or "lovely" is portrayed simply by combining the character for "woman" and for "child".

Just as charming is the combination of the "woman" character under the "roof" character to mean "peace."

WEDNESDAY — MAY 30

MR. McLean says he knows it is spring when he sees the farmers *and* the golfers out plowing.

THURSDAY — MAY 31

NOBODY knows what conscience is, but few people have ever denied that humans possess one. Here are some remarks on the subject:

> There is no witness so terrible,
> no accuser so potent, as the
> CONSCIENCE that dwells in every
> man's breast.
> — *Polybus*

> A good CONSCIENCE enlists a multitude of friends, a bad CONSCIENCE is distressed and anxious, even when alone.
> —*Seneca, The Younger*

> A peace above all earthly dignities,
> A still and quiet CONSCIENCE.
> — *William Shakespeare*

> The moral sense, or CONSCIENCE, is as much part of man as his leg or arm.
> — *Thomas Jefferson*

> CONSCIENCE, the inner voice which warns you that someone may be looking.
> — *H. L. Mencken*

JUNE

FRIDAY — JUNE 1

THIS is the traditional month for marriages.
My own wedding to George took place on this date, and I would like to offer a tribute to marriage by one of the greatest men of this century, Sir Winston Churchill:

"My marriage was much the most fortunate and joyous event which happened to me in my whole life; for what can be more glorious than to be united in one's walk through life with a being incapable of an ignoble thought."

SATURDAY — JUNE 2

MY son-in-law John loves to tell this little story:

He called his daughter into his study one evening to discuss her poor report card. Frances listened gravely and then asked, "What do you think the problem is, Dad — heredity or environment?"

His daughter's unexpected question completely dissolved the "stern" father's annoyance.

SUNDAY — JUNE 3

IT is better to hear the rebuke of the wise than for a man to hear the song of fools.

MONDAY — JUNE 4

I just returned from a visit to Ottawa. It is certainly one of the prettiest capitals in the world, with thousands of flowers in bloom at this time of the year. Did you know that Holland's Queen Juliana donated the first tulip bulbs which bloom in Ottawa each spring as thanks for the kindness shown to her and her family when they lived there during World War II? It was also a gift to honor the Canadian soldiers who helped liberate Holland during the war. What better expression of gratitude.

TUESDAY — JUNE 5

COURAGE is the human virtue that counts most — courage to act on limited knowledge and insufficient evidence. That's all any of us have, so we must have the courage to go ahead and act on a hunch. It's the best we can do.

— *Robert Frost*

WEDNESDAY — JUNE 6

AN excellent recipe for longevity is this: "Cultivate a minor ailment and take good care of it," according to Sir William Osler.

I'm sure my grandmother knew this. She always complained of aches in her elbows, and lived a long, laughing life. She once met Sir William and thought him the most wonderful man — next to her husband, of course.

THURSDAY — JUNE 7

THERE are several good protections against temptations, but the surest is cowardice.
— *Mark Twain*

FRIDAY — JUNE 8

AGNES de Mille, the fine American choreographer, tells of first seeing the legendary dancer, Anna Pavlova. "Pavlova," she said, "had looked me in the face and called my name." From that moment on the young de Mille wanted to dance. And she did.

I often wonder how lucky some indecisive young people would be if such a thing were to happen to them. They could begin to get their lives in order.

SATURDAY — JUNE 9

THERE has been another story in the news about "miracle" capsules that will solve all our nutrition problems. But the scientists who invent them must dislike food because they never mention taste. People like my friend Jake who love food would be most unhappy to eat these capsules.

When I hear about food in capsules I am always reminded of the short story — by Stephen Leacock, I believe — about the child who "stuffed" himself on a Christmas dinner of turkey, stuffing, vegetables, gravy, pudding, in the form of one of those miracle capsules.

SUNDAY — JUNE 10

MAKE a joyful noise unto the Lord, all ye lands.

Serve the Lord with gladness: come before his presence with singing.

MONDAY — JUNE 11

IT is not wisdom to be wise
    And on the inward vision close the eyes
But it is wisdom to believe the heart;
Columbus found a world and had no chart.
                      — *George Santayana*

TUESDAY — JUNE 12

THAT God once loved a garden,
　　We learn in Holy Writ;
And seeing gardens in the spring,
I well can credit it.

— *Winifred Mary Letts*

WEDNESDAY—JUNE 13

MY son-in-law John has just returned from Prince Edward Island, where he was attending a conference.

In the window of a small electrical shop he saw this sign: "The hours is until the work isn't."

THURSDAY — JUNE 14

YEARS ago Mavis Turnridge's father-in-law, an atheist, came to live with her and her family after his wife had passed away. Time and again the older man would engage his son in religious arguments. But he always ended them by saying, "Don't delude yourself, son I still don't believe in God."

To which Mavis one day replied, "But Mr. Turnridge, God believes in you." This remark swept away all resistance, and the old man became a regular churchgoer.

FRIDAY — JUNE 15

AT our library yesterday I saw this quote by Aldous Huxley pinned up in the entranceway: "Every man who knows how to read has it in his power to magnify, to multiply the ways in which he exists, to make his life full, significant and interesting." I know that reading is one of the great pleasures in my life and has saved me often during periods of boredom and impatience.

SATURDAY — JUNE 16

YOU have to climb to reach a deep thought.
— *Stanislaw J. Lec*

SUNDAY — JUNE 17

TODAY is Father's Day and I thought of my own father—a minister—who knew how to make life gay and happy without forgetting about duty and responsibility. When I was a small girl he told me often, "You won't be able to enjoy yourself completely if you leave work undone." What a fine man he was and I hope he's having a good time in heaven now that all his work on earth has been done.

MONDAY — JUNE 18

MY sister Sarah sent me this piece of advice from her Maritime home after I had written to her about a certain problem.

"Have you noticed," she wrote, "how shore birds and gulls face into the wind when they are at rest on the beach? It keeps their feathers in perfect position. Face your troubles and don't let them ruffle your feathers."

TUESDAY — JUNE 19

BETTER do kindness near home than go far away to burn incense.

— *Chinese proverb*

WEDNESDAY — JUNE 20

DO you remember as a child the thrill of shopping at the five-and-ten-cent store? F. W. Woolworth opened his first store on this date in 1879 — one-hundred years ago. By the time he died, he owned 1,000 stores and had made a fortune. Nowadays I guess you'd have to open a one-and-two-dollar store. There's not much to buy these days for five and ten cents.

THURSDAY — JUNE 21

PRAISE youth for tearing things apart,
    Toppling the idols, breaking leases;
Then from the upset apple-cart,
Praise oldsters picking up the pieces.
— *Phyllis McGinley*

FRIDAY — JUNE 22

SONGS are thoughts, sung out with the breath when people are moved by great force and ordinary speech no longer suffices. Man is moved just like the ice floe, sailing here and there out in the current. His thoughts are driven by a flowing force when he feels joy, when he feels sorrow. Thoughts can wash over him like a flood, making his blood come in gasps, and his heart throb.

Something, like an abatement in the weather, will keep him thawed up, and then it will happen that we, who always thought we are small, will feel even smaller. And we will fear to use words. But it will happen that the words we need will come of themselves. When the words we want to use shoot up by themselves — we get a new song.

— *Orpingalik*

SATURDAY — JUNE 23

WE all live under the same sky, but we don't all have the same horizon.

— *Konrad Adenauer*

SUNDAY — JUNE 24

AND Jesus increased in wisdom and stature, and in favor with God and man.

MONDAY — JUNE 25

A remarkable woman runs a nut shop in a village not far from here and has done so for many years.

Recently a customer came in and asked for a quarter pound of nuts. The woman weighed the amount and started to put the nuts into a bag.

"Hey," said the customer, "aren't you going to give me a little more?"

"I gave you what you wanted," she replied.

"Come on. Just a little more."

"Now listen here," she said. "You got what you wanted, fair and square. I'm not in business to give nuts away, you know."

She's a bit brusque, but I do admire her honesty. I wouldn't be surprised to discover that she's a Scot.

TUESDAY — JUNE 26

YESTERDAY afternoon my neighbor's young daughter Maureen dropped in for a visit. During our conversation she remarked that she was unhappy because her birthday was at the end of the month when most of her school friends were away on vacation and unable to celebrate with her. I suggested that she find someone like Robert Louis Stevenson who once drew up a document formally donating his birthday to Annie Ide, a friend's daughter who hated her Christmas birthday. Maureen thought it was a marvelous idea and is all set to find a donor for a new birthday.

WEDNESDAY — JUNE 27

MY elderly aunt once gave me this prescription for a long and healthy life. "Go to bed the same day you get up."

THURSDAY — JUNE 28

AND, of course, it may be that all I have been telling you is wrong. For you cannot be certain about a thing you cannot see. And people say so much!

— *Ikinilik*

FRIDAY — JUNE 29

MY niece Linda just started a summer job in the local newspaper office. She told me that when she applied for the position, the editor said to her, "You won't find any sex discrimination here — everyone's overworked."

SATURDAY — JUNE 30

DO you own the lands? In England, in France, the French and the English have land, the first who were in England, they were the owners of the soil and they transmitted to generations. Now by the soil they have had their start as a nation. Who starts the nations? The very same one who creates them, God. God is the master of the universe, our planet is his land, and the nations, the tribes are members of his family, and as a good Father he gives a portion of his lands to that nation, to that tribe, to everyone, that is his heritage, that is his share of the inheritance, of the people, or nation or tribe.

— *Louis Riel*
Métis leader of the
Red River Rebellion

JULY

ON this July 1, Canada's 112th birthday, I hope that Canadians everywhere will heed the words of a prayer by the gentle Saint Francis:

O God, make us patient and pitiful one with another in the fret and jar of life, remembering that each fights a hard fight and walks a lonely way.

Forgive us, Lord, if we hurt our fellow souls; teach us a gentler tone, a sweeter charity of words, and a more healing touch.

Sustain us, O God, when we must face sorrow; give us courage for the day and hope for the morrow. Day unto day may we lay hold of Thy hand and look into Thy face, whatever befall, until our work is finished and the day is done.

MONDAY — JULY 2

THE nineteenth-century poet George Frederick Cameron wrote some stirring words about freedom. Since this week Canadians are celebrating their nation's birthday and Americans are celebrating Independence Day it may be a good time to remember Cameron's lines:

MY POLITICAL FAITH

I am not of those fierce, wild wills,
Albeit from loins of warlike line,
To wreck laws human and divine
Alike, that on a million ills
I might erect one sacred shrine.

To Freedom: nor again am I
Of these who could be sold and bought
To fall before a Juggernaut:
I hold all "royal right" a lie —
Save that a royal soul hath wrought!

It is in the extreme begins
And ends all danger: if the Few
Would feel, or if the Many knew
This fact, the mass of fewer sins
Would shrive them in their passing through.

TUESDAY — JULY 3

I can see how it might be possible for a man to look down upon the earth and be an atheist, but I cannot conceive how he could look up into the heavens and say there is no God.

— *Abraham Lincoln*

WEDNESDAY — JULY 4

ON this "Glorious Fourth" I think these lovely lines by Susanna Moodie are a fitting tribute to our neighbors to the South and to American people everywhere as they celebrate Independence Day with flags and parades, family outings and family gatherings.

Beautiful — most beautiful in her rugged grandeur is this vast country. How awful is the sublime solitude of her pathless woods! What eloquent thoughts flow out of the deep silence that broods over them! We feel as if we stood alone in the presence of God, and nature lay at his feet in speechless adoration.

THURSDAY — JULY 5

I remember reading years ago on the business page of a newspaper that all too often the clever girl in the office who knows all the answers is never asked.

Times have indeed changed. She's now asking the questions, and young women like my granddaughters have many opportunities open to them. But they also have to make more decisions and have to face many more conflicts, I am afraid.

FRIDAY — JULY 6

MY father used to recite this poem to me when I was a child. For me it typifies summer and youth.

A BOY'S SONG

Where the pools are bright and deep,
Where the gray trout lies asleep,
Up the river and over the lea,
That's the way for Billie and me.

Where the blackbird sings the latest,
Where the hawthorn blooms the sweetest,
Where the nestlings chirp and flee,
That's the way for Billie and me.

SATURDAY — JULY 7

DURING inspection at a Cub camp near here, the counselor found a large umbrella obviously not one of the items listed, stuffed into the bedroll of my grand-nephew. The counselor asked for an explanation. Young Benjamin neatly provided one: "Sir, did you ever have a mother?"

SUNDAY — JULY 8

FOR, thou wilt light my candle, the Lord my God will enlighten my darkness.

MONDAY — JULY 9

SOMETIMES we tend to forget how technology does make certain things in life easier. Yesterday when I went to get the afternoon paper, I found a young woman standing on my porch listening to a tape recorder: "The next house on the right, the house across the street with the blue door . . . " "I'm Billie's mother," she explained. "He's away at camp for the next two weeks and he taped his route for me because I'm delivering his papers for him." I was impressed, I must admit.

TUESDAY — JULY 10

EVERYONE should examine his own conduct, then he will be able to take the measure of his own worth; no need to compare himself with others.

WEDNESDAY — JULY 11

LUNENBURG, Nova Scotia, is a lovely spot, famous for its fishing fleet. My neighbors down the street have just brought me a lovely present from Lunenburg; some fresh fish, which Jake and I will eat later this evening, and a photograph of the historic sailing ship, the *Bluenose*. Goodness, how well I remember watching that first sailing race — as if it were yesterday.

THURSDAY — JULY 12

VISITING a hospital ward one day, the late Queen Mary paused at the bed of a little boy. She asked him where he lived, and the child said, in Battersea, a poor district of London.

"And where do you live?" the boy asked, unaware that his visitor was a queen.

"Oh, just in back of a department store," Queen Mary replied.

FRIDAY — JULY 13

"THERE ain't much fun in medicine, but there's a good deal of medicine in fun."
— *Josh Billings*

My doctor is fond of this little piece of advice. He will be pleased that I have passed it along to my readers.

SATURDAY — JULY 14

LIFE is like an onion; you pull off one layer at a time and sometimes you weep.

SUNDAY — JULY 15

FOR the Lord thy God bringeth thee into a good land, a land of brooks of water, of fountains and depths that spring out of valleys and hills;

A land of wheat, and barley, and vines, and fig trees, and pomegranates; a land of olive oil, and honey;

A land wherein thou shalt eat bread without scarceness, thou shalt not lack any thing in it; a land whose stones are iron, and out of whose hills thou mayest dig brass.

When thou hast eaten and are full, then thou shalt bless the Lord thy God for the good land which he hath given thee.

MONDAY — JULY 16

MY daughter Margaret, feeling devilish no doubt, gave this verse by Daniel Defoe to our minister yesterday:

Wherever God erects a house of prayer,
The Devil always builds a chapel there;
And 'twill be found, upon examination,
The latter has the largest congregation.

Our minister laughed, explaining that his mother was a descendant of the great English moralist.

TUESDAY — JULY 17

IT'S maddening to meet someone who thinks he is superior — and even worse to find out he really is.

WEDNESDAY — JULY 18

JAKE said over tea the other afternoon, "You know we're all inclined to judge ourselves by our ideals, while others we judge by their acts."

I was so impressed with his insight that I congratulated him. To my surprise Jake insisted it wasn't his. He had heard the remark on the radio. Of course, it doesn't matter *where* we hear things, but how we apply them to our own lives.

THURSDAY — JULY 19

MY mother believed in the Golden Rule and tried to live by it. But she had a second maxim, which she called her Iron Rule: "Don't do for others what they wouldn't take the trouble to do for themselves." It's not a bad rule to remember if certain members of the household tend to be sloppy.

FRIDAY — JULY 20

WHEN people complain that their particular lot must surely be the worst, I often think of the words of the Greek philosopher Socrates.

If all our misfortunes were laid in one common heap, whence every one must take an equal portion, most people would be content to take their own and depart.

SATURDAY — JULY 21

IF seeds in the black earth can turn into such beautiful roses, what might not the heart of man become in the long journey toward the stars?

— *G. K. Chesterton*

SUNDAY — JULY 22

IT is a good thing to give thanks unto the Lord, and to sing praises unto thy name, O Most High:

To show forth thy loving-kindness in the morning, and thy faithfulness every night,

Upon an instrument of ten strings, and upon the psaltery; upon the harp with a solemn sound.

For thou, Lord, hast made me glad through thy work: I will triumph in the works of thy hands.

MONDAY — JULY 23

WHEN my son-in-law John recently visited Beirut he was very frightened by the speed and nonchalance of Lebanon's cab drivers. When he questioned a driver about this, the cabby explained, "It shouldn't surprise you. All the bad drivers are dead."

TUESDAY — JULY 24

THE days are very warm, and many people are bothered by the heat. Sometimes a lukewarm shower helps me cool off, but a simpler method is to soak your hands and forearms in cool water. Try it. You will find it most refreshing.

WEDNESDAY — JULY 25

DOCTORS are telling us these days that old age develops a creative urge and power all its own, which we are only just beginning to understand.

Heavens, my friends and I could tell these doctors a thing or two. My brother, for one, took up gardening late in life—in his seventies, I believe—and became so expert that he used to give talks on the radio about raising flowers and plants. Every now and again I meet someone who remembers the good advice he used to give.

THURSDAY — JULY 26

SCENE: A political rally. The crowd is large and Agnes Macphail, the first woman elected to the Canadian House of Commons, is speaking. She is interrupted by a heckler.

Heckler: Don't you wish you were a man?

Macphail: Yes. Don't *you*?

FRIDAY — JULY 27

NO foundation for a house like wisdom, no buttress like discernment, no furnishings may be found for the rooms of it, so rare and pleasant as true knowledge.

SATURDAY — JULY 28

AT prayer one evening, the congregation was asked:

"Am I intolerant of other people and opinions that differ from my own?

Am I prepared to concede that others have a right to their own beliefs and ways of doing things? In short, can I live and let live?"

Such reflections are a good preparation for **Sunday churchgoing.**

SUNDAY — JULY 29

EVERY wise woman buildeth her home: but the foolish plucketh it down with her hands.

He that walketh in his uprightness feareth the Lord: but he that is perverse in his ways despiseth him.

In the mouth of the foolish is a rod of pride: but the lips of the wise shall preserve them.

Where no oxen are, the crib is clean: but much increase is by the strength of the ox.

MONDAY — JULY 30

ACCORDING to the great 18th-century German dramatist and philosopher Johann Wolfgang von Goethe there are nine requisites for contented living:

HEALTH enough to make work a pleasure

WEALTH enough to support your needs

STRENGTH enough to battle with difficulties and overcome them

GRACE enough to confess your sins and forsake them

PATIENCE enough to toil until some good is accomplished

CLARITY enough to see some good in your neighbor

LOVE enough to move you to be useful and helpful to others

FAITH enough to make real the things of God

HOPE enough to remove all anxious fears concerning the future.

TUESDAY — JULY 31

EVERYBODY, soon or late, sits down to a banquet of consequences.

— *Robert Louis Stevenson*

AUGUST

WEDNESDAY — AUGUST 1

HERE is an amusing verse by Edward **Lear**
to start off the month:
There was an Old Man of Quebec,
A beetle ran over his neck;
But he cried, "With a needle
I'll slay you O beadle!"
That angry Old Man of Quebec.

THURSDAY — AUGUST 2

WALKING is the easiest way people **have**
ever invented to escape boredom.

FRIDAY — AUGUST 3

HALF a dozen of us were standing in line at
the checkout counter, when suddenly the
cash register went haywire. Clicking wildly, it
rang up the same amount a first, a second, a
third time . . . . As the clerk gazed helplessly at
the machine, I heard a voice behind me ex-
claim: "Heavens! These prices are too much
even for the machinery!"

SATURDAY — AUGUST 4

CHARM is the ability to make somebody feel that both of you are pretty wonderful.

SUNDAY — AUGUST 5

ALL I have seen teaches me to trust the Creator for all I have not seen.

— *Ralph Waldo Emerson*

MONDAY — AUGUST 6

YESTERDAY was Sunday, so I saved for today this heroic statement by Sir Alexander Mackenzie, the great explorer.

When he arrived at Bella Coola, British Columbia, the first European to do so, he wrote:

"I now mixed up some vermilion in melted grease, and inscribed in large characters, on the South-East face of the rock . . . .
Alexander Mackenzie, seventeen hundred and ninety-three."

How my patriotic heart jumped when I first read those words!

TUESDAY — AUGUST 7

"OLD age," said Stephen Leacock, "is the 'front line' of life, moving into no-man's land. No-man's land is covered with mist. Beyond it is eternity."

Since Leacock's day, we have learned a lot about life and aging. No longer do we think about front lines and no-man's land. "Instead," as Jake is fond of saying, "we have a d. . . good time."

WEDNESDAY — AUGUST 8

AFTER listening to Muriel's friend, Sally Crawford talk and talk about good conversation, Muriel and I concluded that being a good conversationalist had nothing to do with the ability to talk but rather with the ability to listen. And we realized that too few of us know how to listen.

THURSDAY — AUGUST 9

A lady visiting George Bernard Shaw was surprised not to find any flowers in his home. "I thought you were fond of flowers," she said. "I am," Shaw replied. "I'm also fond of children, but I don't cut off their heads and stick them in pots around the house."

FRIDAY — AUGUST 10

THERE can be no true satisfaction in life if the things we believe in are different from the things we do.

SATURDAY — AUGUST 11

MY granddaughter Phyllis found this passage and thought my readers might enjoy it. It comes from a seventeenth-century pamphlet, *Haec Mulier* ("This Woman"), in which an Englishwoman proudly declares:

We are as free-born as men, have as free election, and as free spirits. We are compounded of like parts, and may with like liberty make benefit of our creations: my countenance shall smile on the worthy and frown on the ignoble. I will hear the wise and be deaf to idiots; give counsel to my friends, but be dumb to flatterers. I have hands that shall be liberal to reward desert, feet that shall move swiftly to do good office, and thoughts that shall ever accompany freedom and severity.

SUNDAY — AUGUST 12

THUS cleansed I them from all strangers, and appointed the wards of the priests and Levites, every one in his business;

And for the wood offering, at times appointed, and for the first fruits. Remember me, O my God, for good.

MONDAY — AUGUST 13

MANY, many years ago an Oblate missionary was trying to convert a Dogrib Indian by explaining the joys of heaven. The Indian was skeptical.

"Tell me," he said, "is it like the land of the little trees when the ice has left the lakes? Are the great musk oxen there? Are the hills covered with flowers? There will I see the caribou everywhere I look? Are the lakes blue with the sky of summer? Is every net full of great, fat whitefish? Is there room for me in this land, like our land, the Barrens? Can I camp anywhere and not find that someone else has camped? Can I feel the wind and be like the wind? Father, if your Heaven is not all these, leave me alone in my land, the land of the little sticks."

TUESDAY — AUGUST 14

TO be wronged is nothing, unless you continue to remember it.

— Confucius

WEDNESDAY — AUGUST 15

HAIL August: Maiden of the sultry days,
  To thee I bring the measured need of
    praise.
  For, though thou hast besmirched the
    day and night,
  And hid a wealth of glory from our
    sight,
  Thou still dost build in musing,
    pensive mood,
  Thy blissful idylls in the underwood.

  Thou still dost yield new beauties,
    fair and young,
  With many a form of grace as yet
    unsung,
  Which ripens o'er thy pathway and
    repays
  The toil and languor of the sultry
    days.

— Charles Mair

THURSDAY — AUGUST 16

"WHY do ants crawl like this?" asked three-year-old Christopher as he scampered across the floor on all fours. "Why don't they go like this?" And he moved slowly backwards, grinning at his mother.

Nonplussed, she replied, "Because they don't have toes."

FRIDAY — AUGUST 17

FRIENDS of mine were standing shivering in a cold rain at an isolated suburban bus stop in Calgary one Sunday morning. Car after car passed. Then a battered old truck stopped, the door opened, and a cracked voice shouted, "Get in!"

They did gladly. The elderly driver asked where they were going.

"To church."

"Thought so. This is a taxi, you know."

On seeing the look of surprise on their faces, he explained. "Yep—the Good Samaritan taxi. Been operating it for sixteen years. Never charged a cent. I get a kick out of meeting people, and it gives *me* a lift, too."

And he drove my friends to the church—five miles away.

SATURDAY — AUGUST 18

MASAKA Wade is a charming Japanese my granddaughter Phyllis recently introduced to me. He told me that as a student in Japan he was too poor to buy books.

"So I often picked up a book and read it in the store, sometimes returning day after day to finish it. There was one book I wanted so badly that I finally borrowed the money from a friend to buy it. But when I went back to the store, I found it had been put on a shelf marked 'Reserved.' Disappointed, I explained the circumstances to the storekeeper.

" 'We put the book on reserve,' he said with a smile, 'because we did not want to sell it before you got through with it. A book is there to be read, even if it has to be read in the store.' "

Jake who had also been listening to the young man's story was impressed. Whether he would encourage similar practices in his own bookstore is something I hesitated to ask him.

SUNDAY — AUGUST 19

BETTER a humble lot among peaceful folk, than all the spoils a tyrant's friendship can bring you.

MONDAY — AUGUST 20

MY son-in-law Bruce is laid up with aching muscles and joints. Like many middle-aged men, he has been bitten by the jogging bug. Now, I have no objection to such an exercise, but few people seem aware that they must be ready for it.

"If you are searching for good health and fitness," I told Bruce, "you can keep your weight down by not overeating, by getting enough sleep, and by having frequent vacations." He will just as easily live a long, fit life if he takes a leisurely walk every day.

TUESDAY — AUGUST 21

"ONE humiliating thing about technology is that it is gradually filling our homes with appliances smarter than we are." said a fashionably dressed young man on television last evening.

Such remarks make me very angry. There's no doubt we have many intricate machines, but to consider them "smart" is misusing words. Besides, no one insists that the young man—or anyone else—buy them. What people like him need is a little common sense. I would say to him, "Think before you speak."

WEDNESDAY — AUGUST 22

CHARLES Mair was an astute observer of nature. Here are some more lines from his poem "August:"

> *. . . When all the woods*
> *Grow dim with smoke, and smirch*
> *   their lively green*
> *With haze of long-continued*
> *   drought begot;*
> *When every field grows yellow,*
> *   and a plague*
> *Of thirst dries up its herbage*
> *   to the root,*
> *So that the cattle grow quite*
> *   ribby-lean*
> *On woody stalks whose juices*
> *   all are spent;*
> *When every fronded fern in mid-wood*
> *   heat,*
> *Grows sick and yellow with the*
> *   jaundice heat,*
> *Whilst those on hill-sides glare*
> *   with patchy red;*
> *When streamlets die upon the*
> *   lichened rocks,*
> *And leave the bleaching pebbles*
> *   shining bare . . .*

THURSDAY — AUGUST 23

DAVID Jenkins, a student friend of my grandson Robert tells this story about London's famous Hyde Park Corner.

Many years ago, when traffic was not as heavy as it is today at the Corner, a man was driving past in an old noisy car. He stopped to listen to a little man, who was denouncing the Royal Family.

Soon a police constable appeared, and the man fully expected the orator to be arrested, or told to move along. Instead the bobby came over to the man in the car and asked him very politely: "Would you mind turning off your motor, so everyone can hear what the speaker is saying?"

FRIDAY — AUGUST 24

"CURIOSITY," Arnold Edinborough once concluded, "is the very basis of education; and if you tell me that curiosity killed the cat, I say the cat died nobly."

SATURDAY — AUGUST 25

ABOUT criticism an Arab philosopher said: "If you stop every time a dog barks, your journey will never end."

SUNDAY — AUGUST 26

LORD, thou hast been our dwelling place in all generations.

Before the mountains were brought forth, Or ever thou hadst formed the earth and the world, Even from everlasting to everlasting, thou art God.

MONDAY — AUGUST 27

WALKING, as you must have heard me say before, is for all seasons. Yesterday I took my son-in-law Bruce on a short walk, because his leg muscles still bother him.

But we walked long enough to see the abundant flowers, to watch children at play, and hear the birds singing happily one to another —even, every now and again, to see the occasional colored leaf.

Signs of autumn come earlier now.

TUESDAY — AUGUST 28

THIS notice on the church bulletin board amused me: "A new loudspeaker has been installed in the church. It was given by one of the members in memory of his wife."

WEDNESDAY — AUGUST 29

TO keep well by too strict a regimen is a tedious disease in itself.

— *La Rochefoucauld*

THURSDAY — AUGUST 30

MY four-year-old great-grandson—goodness, another generation!—is fascinated with airplanes. Every time one flies over the house, he rushes to the window to watch until it becomes a speck in the distance.

Last week he had his first ride, on a plane to Halifax. Of course, Geoffrey was terribly excited about the flight. Ten or fifteen minutes into it, he looked around, turned to his mother, and asked expectantly, "When do we start to get smaller, Mommy?"

FRIDAY — AUGUST 31

"GOD has made Canada one of those nations which cannot be conquered and cannot be destroyed—except by itself." When I read those lines I begin to wonder what we can do to preserve our heritage. Some of the stories I read in the newspaper make me realize that it is up to us to conserve the environment.

SEPTEMBER

SATURDAY — SEPTEMBER 1

SEPTEMBER is when millions of shining, happy faces turn toward school. They belong to mothers.

SUNDAY — SEPTEMBER 2

BLESSED art thou, O Lord, teach me to know thy will. By these lips let the awards thou makest ever be recorded. Blithely as one that has found great possessions, I follow thy decrees.

MONDAY — SEPTEMBER 3

FOR me, September has always been more the beginning of the year than January. I guess it dates back to my childhood when September meant the beginning of school, a new grade, a new teacher, and new clothes and shoes to start off the school year. Even though I have been out of school for many, many years, I still feel a tingle of anticipation at the beginning of this month.

TUESDAY — SEPTEMBER 4

MY friend Emily from Philadelphia has just returned from a trip to the Holy Land and was very impressed by a ceremony she was lucky enough to witness there. When young Israeli workers go out to plant new trees which are vital factors in soil conservation, improvement of climate, and the extension of habitable areas, they joyously sing the following song, reminiscent of songs sung in Old Testament times:

We shall plant;
On hill, in vale, at ocean strand,
Spreading forest's greening stand,
We shall plant.

In ancient times, at birth of child,
They did plant;
Cypress bark and cedar wild,
Carobs broad and olives mild
They did plant.

Our nation now is born anew,
So we plant;
On wastes of sand which deserts blew
In deadly swamps of somber hue,
There we plant.

WEDNESDAY — SEPTEMBER 5

MY neighbor sent her small son off to his first day of school this week. When she asked him how many children were in his class he replied, with all the dignity of his age, "There are 14. Seven boys and about a million girls."

THURSDAY — SEPTEMBER 6

TO be nameless in worthy deeds exceeds an infamous history . . . Who had not rather been the good thief, than Pilate?
— *Thomas Browne*

FRIDAY — SEPTEMBER 7

I sometimes think that the idea of discipline was dropped too quickly by modern parents and teachers, perhaps because they themselves had suffered from an approach that was too harsh.

Eleanor Roosevelt once remarked how she was able to get through some of the bad periods of her later life. "Because of the early discipline I received, I inevitably grew into a really tough person." And, I might add, one of the greatest women of her time.

SATURDAY — SEPTEMBER 8

MY granddaughter Phyllis's friend Mary teaches high school. She said the highlight of opening day occurred when one of the teachers sent in her attendance report. It read, "Help! They're all here!"

SUNDAY — SEPTEMBER 9

BELIEVE me, you have only to make any request of the Father in my name, and He will grant it to you.

MONDAY — SEPTEMBER 10

YESTERDAY our minister gave a sermon on love. He said that he had always disliked the phrase "falling in love," because of the word "fall." It implied, he said, that we are walking along calmly when we suddenly come across a hole and fall in. He explained that real love always takes time, just as a seed planted today does not grow overnight into a flower but needs proper nourishment to achieve its full beauty. I hope some of the younger members of the congregation were listening. But I suspect that youth always will, and perhaps must, *fall in love.* It's part of **growing up.**

Tuesday — September 11

A single sunbeam is enough to drive away many shadows.

— *St. Francis of Assisi*

Wednesday — September 12

LAST night my neighbors, the Clarkes, gave a party. Their youngest daughter Kelly, aged nine, was desperate to stay up to see the guests. Okay, said her parents. As it was a cool evening, she would have to look after the guests' coats. She agreed.

Without her parents noticing it, Kelly took a saucer from the kitchen, placed a dime on it, and put it on a small table near the front closet.

By the end of the evening she had collected $3.75.

This morning her parents are furious, but were somewhat mollified when Kelly explained that the money was going to a fund to help homeless animals.

Thursday — September 13

A decent provision for the poor is the true test of civilization.

— *Samuel Johnson*

Friday — September 14

HERE are some thoughts from earlier times on activity and prayer:

Activity is better than inertia. Act, but with self-control. . . . The world is imprisoned in its own activity, except when actions are performed as worship of God.

— *The Bhagavad-Gita*

It is by our power to stretch out our arms and, by doing good in actions, to seize life and set it in our soul.

— *Origen*

Actions are right in proportion as they tend to promote happiness; wrong as they tend to produce the reverse of happiness.

— *John Stuart Mill*

We have left undone those things which we ought to have done; and have done those things which we ought not to have done.

— *Book of Common Prayer*

SATURDAY — SEPTEMBER 15

WE suppose there is hardly a man who has not an apple orchard locked away in his heart somewhere.

— *Christopher Morley*

I know that I have one in mine. Many an hour as a child I lay under an apple tree in my father's orchard, reading a book and being completely happy.

I don't think watching television can ever replace that pure and serene joy I experienced being out in the fresh air, listening to the birds singing, and, indeed, feeling that all was right with my particular world.

SUNDAY — SEPTEMBER 16

YOU are the light of the world; a city cannot be hidden if it is built on a mountain top.

A lamp is not lighted to be put away under a bushel measure; it is put on a lamp stand to give light to all the people of the house, and your light must shine so brightly before men that they can see good works and glorify your Father who is in heaven.

MONDAY — SEPTEMBER 17

JAKE dropped over last night, and when we were sitting on the porch he suddenly said, "You know, Edna, autumn is widely believed to be a melancholic time of the year, but it has its compensations." "What are they, Jake?" I asked. "Why, you can accept a dinner invitation with a fifty-fifty chance that you will get to eat indoors," he said.

TUESDAY — SEPTEMBER 18

THE oldest short words — Yes and No — are those which require the most thought.
— *Pythagoras*

WEDNESDAY — SEPTEMBER 19

MY niece was very put off by her boss this week because he left until the very last moment a job he knew had to be done—and then rushed her.

Thoroughly provoked, she told him she would like to be boss for just one week and let him be the secretary. His reply gave her cause for thought.

"It wouldn't work," he said crisply, "I could never drink that much coffee."

THURSDAY — SEPTEMBER 20

HERE are some thoughts for today sent along by some of my readers:

What's so remarkable about love at first sight? It's when people have been looking at each other for years that it becomes remarkable.

You probably wouldn't worry about what people think if you could know how seldom they do.

Wisdom is in knowing when to speak your mind and when to mind your speech.

Prayer is a time exposure of the soul to God.

FRIDAY — SEPTEMBER 21

IN law, a man is guilty when he violates the rights of another. In ethics, he is guilty if he only thinks of doing so.

— Immanuel Kant

SATURDAY — SEPTEMBER 22

MRS. Shea, a parishioner I've known for years, is not exactly happy about Mr. Shea's decision to retire from his job earlier than he had originally intended. "I'll tell you what retirement is," she said on the church steps last Sunday, "retirement is when he putters around the house and mutters around the yard."

SUNDAY — SEPTEMBER 23

LORD, thy mercy is as high as heaven, thy faithfulness reaches to the clouds; thy justice stands firm as the everlasting hills; the wisdom of thy decrees is deep as the abyss.

MONDAY — SEPTEMBER 24

DID you know that the word *humor* originally meant moisture or juice? Only in the seventeenth century did the word come to mean that quality of action, speech, or writing which excites amusement. But everyone who has experienced the lubricating effect of a small joke realizes that humor still has an element of "juice." It keeps life from drying up and losing its flavor.

TUESDAY — SEPTEMBER 25

IT isn't life that matters, but the courage we bring to it.

— *Hugh Walpole*

WEDNESDAY — SEPTEMBER 26

HAROLD Nicolson once said that he regarded sloth as the major cause of melancholy in that it provoked a sense of inadequacy and therefore guilt leading finally to fear. He went on to say that "melancholy is caused less by the failure to achieve great ambitions or desires than by the inability to perform small, necessary acts."

A retired physician, writer, and philologist, Dr. Percy Friedenberg, who died at age 92, also said, "Nothing ages you and tires you as much as inactivity, and the avoidance of rest is one of the things that enables you to go on in old age."

THURSDAY — SEPTEMBER 27

ADAM ate the apple and our teeth still ache.

— *Hungarian proverb*

Friday — September 28

PRAY to God, but row for shore.

— *Russian proverb*

Saturday — September 29

MY brother and sister-in-law had different religious beliefs and delighted in arguing various points. I once visited them for the weekend, and the morning after a long and lively discussion I asked Marie who had won.

"No one ever wins," she explained. "After all, there are no definite answers. Your brother could be as right as I am, or I could be as wrong as he is."

Sunday — September 30

IT is faith that lets us understand how the worlds were fashioned by God's work: how it was from things unseen that the things we see took their origin.

OCTOBER

MONDAY — OCTOBER 1

A friend, Mavis Tewbury from Winnipeg sent me this recipe:

HOW TO LIVE HAPPILY

Take two heaping cups of patience, one heartful of love, and two handfuls of generosity. Add a dash of laughter and a full cup of understanding plus two cups of loyalty. Mix well and sprinkle generously with kindness. Spread this irresistible delicacy over a lifetime and serve everybody you meet.

TUESDAY — OCTOBER 2

THE famous financier Bernard Baruch was once asked what his rules for success in business were. Here's the list he gave:
- Be quick to praise people.
- Be polite.
- Be helpful.
- Be cheerful.
- Don't be envious.

WEDNESDAY — OCTOBER 3

THOSE griefs smart most which are seen to be of our own choice.

— *Sophocles*

THURSDAY — OCTOBER 4

MY friend Marcia from Boston has been worried lately about the prospect of selling her house. She wrote to me that she had fretted for days as to whether or not to sell her home of the past 30 years, now that her children have left.

Finally, she got herself so upset she decided she had to take her mind off the problem. She set about cleaning, decorating, and overhauling the old house. She discovered that the exercise not only made her stop worrying but that after a month or so of repairs and decorating the house looked so lovely and inviting, she knew she didn't want to part with it. She decided to stay put and rent a few rooms to college students.

Exercise is often the antidote to worry. If we used our muscles more and our brains less, I think we'd all be as surprised as Marcia with the results.

FRIDAY — OCTOBER 5

DOUBTS are far more cruel than the worst of truths.

— *Molière*

SATURDAY — OCTOBER 6

I have a good friend who visits the sick, the old, and the friendless. Her small house is always full of visitors who drop in unannounced and stay for hours, or even days. Young mothers drop off their children without notice, and ask my friend to babysit.

And yet I've never heard her complain about being taken advantage of. After one particular imposition which annoyed me, I blurted out, "The way everybody uses you makes me mad!"

She looked at me with pleased surprise and said simply, "I'm so glad you get mad for me, Edna, I simply don't have the time."

SUNDAY — OCTOBER 7

THERE is no embalming like a good name left behind; man's true birthday is the day of his death, which he desires for himself.

MONDAY — OCTOBER 8

BECAUSE this is the day Canada celebrates Thanksgiving Day, I would like to offer this quote from Helen Keller: "For three things I thank God every day of my life; thanks that he has vouchsafed me knowledge of his works; deep thanks that he has set in my darkness the lamp of faith; deep, deepest thanks that I have another life to look forward to—a life with light, flowers, and heavenly song."

Surely if Miss Keller could find it in her heart to give thanks despite her terrible handicaps, the rest of us should find it easy to praise God for our blessings.

TUESDAY — OCTOBER 9

OCTOBER is my favorite month because of certain delights only to be found during this time of the year. October is a brisk wind in the colored leaves, a gleam from a jack-o'-lantern, laughter under a full moon.

October is the sound of geese honking in their flight south, a full jam closet, long evenings with a book beside a fire.

October is deer eating windfalls in the orchard, the bark of the courting fox, and the year come to harvest.

WEDNESDAY — OCTOBER 10

ETHEL Smythe, a long-time neighbor, was shocked at the high price of apples in the supermarket and complained to the manager. "They're pricey, all right," he said, "but that's because apples are scarce." Ethel was astonished. The crop had been so great that apples were rotting in the trees. "That's just it, ma'am. Apples are scarce, because it just doesn't pay to pick 'em." Angry at such waste, Ethel and several friends drove to an orchard outside town and spent the afternoon picking apples.

THURSDAY — OCTOBER 11

FIVE-year-old Beth Robertson was proving a trial to her new teacher. It seems that in art class, Beth would not draw straight lines and circles just as her young teacher wanted. Instead, "Beth draws blobs and funny shapes. I can't understand what's going wrong."

When her mother gently asked all about it, Beth replied quite simply, "I think, and then I draw a line around my think."

FRIDAY — OCTOBER 12

SOMETIMES the pinnacle of fame and the height of folly are twin peaks.

SATURDAY — OCTOBER 13

MY bedridden friend Betty is a wonderful old lady who has more friends than you can imagine. When I asked her what her secret for friendship was, she said: "It's quite simple, I listen. Most people talk right past one another—parents talk past their children, teachers past their students. When people find I am really interested in listening to them, they can hardly believe it. "Of course," she laughed, "it helps to be a little deaf at the right moments." "What moments are those?" I asked. "Oh, when people are mean and spiteful I just tune them out. I tell them I can't hear when they talk about things they'll regret later."

SUNDAY — OCTOBER 14

CONSIDER the ravens: for they neither sow nor reap; which neither have storehouse nor barn; and God feedeth them: how much more are ye better than the fowls?

MONDAY — OCTOBER 15

AGAINST thy lover bear it not in mind if once or twice in life he proves unkind.

— *Sadi*

TUESDAY — OCTOBER 16

WE hear a lot these days about mental health. Here are five ways to determine whether a person is mentally healthy:

1. Have a wide variety of sources of gratification.
2. Be flexible under stress.
3. Recognize and accept limitations and assets.
4. Treat other people as individuals.
5. Be active and productive.

Do *you* have these qualifications?

WEDNESDAY — OCTOBER 17

FRIENDSHIP with a man is friendship with his virtue and does not admit of assumptions of superiority.

— *Mencius*

THURSDAY — OCTOBER 18

I felt dismayed by a difficult task ahead of me this month, when I suddenly remembered my Aunt Lucy.

Years ago, when I was a young girl, we were out walking in the country together. Aunt Lucy suggested we take off our shoes and cross a small river to explore the other side. I raised all sorts of objections: "I'll fall in and get my clothes wet; I'll cut my feet on the stones," etc.

Exasperated, Aunt Lucy finally snapped at me, "Why are you picturing pitfalls where bridges ought to be?" Her words shamed me and we crossed the river without incident to find a meadow near the river full of wild daffodils — a sight I have never forgotten. I decided to start thinking about the "bridges" and move ahead with my project.

FRIDAY — OCTOBER 19

HERE are some thoughts on love I would like to share with you today:
Love is the expansion of two natures in such a fashion that each includes the other, each is enriched by the other.
— *Felix Adler*

SATURDAY — OCTOBER 20

HERE'S a Winston Churchill anecdote sent to me by a friend from Atlanta, Georgia who knows I'm an avid collector of stories about him.

At a dinner party Sir Winston, who was seated across the table from Lady Churchill, kept making his hand walk up and down the table. two fingers bent at the knuckles. The fingers appeared to be walking towards Lady Churchill.

Finally, overcome by curiosity, Lady Churchill's dinner partner asked, "Why is Sir Winston looking at you so wistfully and whatever is he doing with those two knuckles on the table?"

"That's simple," she replied. "We had a mild quarrel before we left home and he's indicating to me it's his fault and he's on his knees in abject apology."

SUNDAY — OCTOBER 21

TWO things must never leave thee, kindness and loyalty; be these the seals that hang about thy neck, graven be this inscription with thy heart for a tablet; so both to God and man thou shalt be friend and confidant.

MONDAY — OCTOBER 22

EVEN the wisest men make fools of themselves about women and even the most foolish woman is wise about men.

— *Theodor Reik*

TUESDAY — OCTOBER 23

AN American visitor in a Montreal restaurant went to the washroom, turned on what he thought was the cold water, and was scalded with hot water. "Why aren't your taps properly marked?" he screamed at the manager.

The manager explained that the tap was marked *C* for *chaud*, which is French for "hot."

The customer stood abashed. Then he made a discovery. "Wait a minute, the other tap is marked *C* too. What about that?"

"But of course," said the proprietor. "That stands for 'cold.' This is a bilingual restaurant in a bilingual city, *mon ami*."

WEDNESDAY — OCTOBER 24

LIFE is a battle in which we fall from the wounds we receive while running away.

— *William L. Sullivan*

THURSDAY — OCTOBER 25

LETTER-writing is the only device for combining solitude and good company.

— *Lord Byron*

FRIDAY — OCTOBER 26

MICKEY'S third-grade teacher, "Old " Conroy, as almost everyone used to call her, has been a firm disciplinarian for twenty years or more.

What has always enraged her was returning to a class and finding her pupils talking and laughing.

One day "Old" Conroy came back to find Mickey's class quiet and peaceful — not a sound. Miss Conroy's jaw dropped. "How did this happen?"

"Well," said a hesitant student at the back of the room, "you told us if ever you left the room and came back to find us all quiet, you'd drop dead."

SATURDAY — OCTOBER 27

IT is not enough for a man to know how to ride; he must also know how to fall.

— *Indian saying*

SUNDAY — OCTOBER 28

DO you understand you are God's temple and that God's spirit has a dwelling in you? If anybody desecrates the temple of God, God will bring him ruin.

MONDAY — OCTOBER 29

MY young grandniece Maureen has just begun to learn classical guitar and is totally absorbed in it. It sometimes worries her mother who fears she may be neglecting her school studies because of this interest. To reassure her, I sent along this quote from the famous Canadian conductor Sir Ernest MacMillan:

"Musicians, more than most people, tend to be introspective and individualistic because of the constant striving for perfection which they share with all true artists."

Maureen's mother wrote back to me and said that if she thought her daughter had some ability as an artist she would feel better; but her playing had not given her any hint of talent so far. In fact, her practicing occurs suspiciously at those hours when she is supposed to do her homework and help with the dishes.

TUESDAY — OCTOBER 30

IT seems to me that parents and teachers to-day give our young people little guidance about attitudes to life and about sex. My generation had little trouble with attitudes to life and to sex, and the reason is quite simple: Unlike parents and teachers today, our parents were quite certain about their attitudes to life and to young people.

WEDNESDAY — OCTOBER 31

TODAY I intend to spend the afternoon making candy apples for the tykes who will come around this evening for "trick or treat." It makes me sad to think that this marvelous holiday for children might be eventually ruined by those few sick people who put pins in apples and hand out poisoned candy. I do not understand why certain people refuse to honor the old customs on Hallowe'en. What could be more enchanting than to see youngsters dressed up, enjoying themselves so hugely on this day which is special for them? I can only guess that certain people have forgotten their own youth, and more's the pity for them.

NOVEMBER

THURSDAY — NOVEMBER 1

IF all our misfortunes were laid in one common heap, whence every one must take an equal portion, most people would be content to take their own and depart.

— *Socrates*

FRIDAY — NOVEMBER 2

WHEN young Alastair came home from work one day and found the house in complete disarray he exclaimed, "What happened?" "Well," his wife Mary told him, "You are always wondering what I do all day. Here it is—I didn't do it."

SATURDAY — NOVEMBER 3

WHEN my son-in-law John visited his childhood home in northern New Hampshire, he learned that the old farmer who used to do odd jobs on the property was dead. As his widow put it, "Pa didn't winter well."

THE HERITAGE BOOK

HERE are two prayers which were sent to me and seem right for the first Sunday in the month.

FOR SERENITY

Slow me down, Lord!

Ease the pounding of my heart by the quieting of my mind.

Steady my hurried pace with the vision of the eternal reach of time.

Give me, amid the confusion of my day, the calmness of the everlasting hills.

Inspire me to send my roots into the soil of life's enduring values that I may grow toward the stars of my greater destiny.

FOR SIMPLICITY

Lord, temper with tranquility
My manifold activity
That I may do my work for Thee
In very great simplicity.

MONDAY — NOVEMBER 5

I am told that the Indians used to welcome the Indian summer days as a last chance to prepare for the cold winter months. How times change! For the past several days we have been blessed with warm sunny weather. No one worries about the coming winter. But I am glad we can still respond to these lines by Wilfred Campbell:

> *Along the line of smokey hills*
> *The crimson forest stands,*
> *And all the day the blue-jay calls*
> *Throughout the autumn lands.*

TUESDAY — NOVEMBER 6

GEORGE had a friend who was a particularly successful contractor. He used to say that he owed his good fortune to the "sidewalk superintendents"—the people who watched his buildings go up.

Alfred used to tell George that he employed one man to do nothing else but listen to the comments of these sidewalk superintendents, and that many a major construction problem was solved by piecing together these bits of wisdom and good advice.

WEDNESDAY — NOVEMBER 7

MELISSA MacDonald enjoys looking for "ploopers" and old sayings. She recently found this epitaph in a Nebraska cemetery.

Here Lies
Ezekiel Aikle
Age 103
The Good
Die Young

THURSDAY — NOVEMBER 8

MY family ancestry is British, Irish, and Scottish. My father was Irish and my mother was a Scot, and there was often teasing between my parents about the various attributes of their respective backgrounds. But I remember best when our family was at a park listening to a Scottish pipe band, music which particularly appealed to my mother. After a half-hour of bagpipes, my father turned to my mother and asked innocently: "Do you know who invented the bagpipes?" "No," my mother replied. "Well," said my father, "it was the Irish. They invented them as a joke and gave them to the Scots, who still haven't seen the joke."

FRIDAY — NOVEMBER 9

AH, a fall morning, crisp as a fresh young apple: rosy on the one side, cool on the other. No wonder so many of my dear friends love a long walk before breakfast.

— Adapted from Anne Morrow Lindbergh

SATURDAY — NOVEMBER 10

IT isn't life that matters, but the courage we bring to it.

— Hugh Walpole

SUNDAY — NOVEMBER 11

WHEN the church bells began to ring, Mrs. Cathcart's great-granddaughter asked, "What are they for?"

"Well, Emilia," replied the old woman, "those bells are to remind us of all those brave young men who died in the wars."

"Who were they?" asked Emilia.

And the old lady began to tell about seeing two sons go off to the first great war, two young sons who never came back. There was silence for a long time, and tears came to the old lady's eyes.

"Oh, Gran," cried Emilia, "I never really understood about war before."

MONDAY — NOVEMBER 12

THREE-year-old Christopher was eating a banana his mother had peeled for him. "Hold it higher, dear, or the banana will fall," she said, meaning, take a better grip. Obediently Christopher raised his arm to shoulder height. "No, hold it higher."

The little fellow's arm shot over his head, and the top two-thirds of the banana slumped to the kitchen floor. His mother had to laugh, but how was her young son to know what she meant?

TUESDAY — NOVEMBER 13

NOTHING is really work unless you would rather be doing something else.
— *Sir James M. Barrie*

WEDNESDAY — NOVEMBER 14

"A man may think he loves his wife because she is beautiful, talented, and competent. But this is not love; it's merely approval." Guess who said that? The suffragette Nellie McClung, more than forty years ago on the Prairies.

THURSDAY — NOVEMBER 15

"DEMOCRACY substitutes self-restraint for external restraint. Democracy demands continuous sacrifice by the individual and more exigent obedience to the moral law than any other form of government."

With these words the famous American jurist, Mr. Justice Brandeis, reminds all of us just how fragile our democratic system of government really is and how easily it could be shattered.

FRIDAY — NOVEMBER 16

YESTERDAY, over tea and cookies, old Mr. Meers and I were talking about the differences between horse-drawn carriages and motor cars.

To my astonishment, Mr. Meers remarked that a horse-drawn carriage used to travel an average of eleven miles an hour in downtown Toronto traffic. Today the average speed of an automobile along these same streets is six miles an hour. Do you think this is progress?

SATURDAY — NOVEMBER 17

OUT shopping one morning in downtown Toronto, I wondered about this sign in a shop window on Queen Street: "Piano Moving. If you have a piano to move, take advantage of our expert service and careful handling." Just underneath that remark was the surprise: "Kindling wood for sale." I don't know whether I would want that firm to move *my* piano.

SUNDAY — NOVEMBER 18

A merry heart doeth good like a medicine.

MONDAY — NOVEMBER 19

MANY friends who belong to my church group have helped organize volunteer services, and June Ragwell tells me the response in the neighborhood has been warm and enthusiastic. Some people, I guess, are helping in order to escape boredom, while others want something to do during the long winter months. Newcomers, of course, will make new friends. But the basic reason for all this generosity, I am convinced, is that most of the volunteers want to serve our community.

TUESDAY — NOVEMBER 20

MY old friend Edith still loves traveling across Canada, and yesterday this post-card arrived from Saskatoon.

> *Stopped for coffee at a shop operated by a blind Vietnam war veteran. Marvelous how he handled everything. When I paid, I told him it was a dollar bill, and he gave me the change. "Do people ever cheat and say a one is a five?" I asked. "No, the only trouble is with people who give me fives and tell me they're ones."*

Restores your faith in people, doesn't it?

WEDNESDAY — NOVEMBER 21

MY granddaughter Phyllis and I were sitting at a lunch counter, and we were having trouble attracting the attention of the waiters. Feeling a bit naughty, Phyllis raised her voice slightly and said, "I do hope that handsome one waits on us, don't you?"

Instantly the three waiters approached us as one man. And they say women are vain!

THURSDAY — NOVEMBER 22

FOR many years, George and I used to drive to Rochester, New York, to spend the American Thanksgiving holiday with the Jacksons. Frank was a Northerner and Sara-May from the South.

Before Thanksgiving they would toss a coin to see whether we would have "Northern" pumpkin pie or "Southern" pecan pie for our dessert. George and I would also have our own little bets as to whether we would be treated to a Southern or Northern menu.

Not only were the Jacksons from different parts of the United States, but also of opposite temperaments. Frank was a pessimist of the worst kind and Sara-May a confirmed optimist.

That year I remember, as soon as we had finished our turkey, candied yams, hushpuppies, grits, and cranberry sauce, George asked, "who won this time?" Frank replied, "nobody did," whereas Sara-May called out from the kitchen "we both did." Seconds later, she walked through the door carrying a pumpkin pie in her right hand and a pecan pie in her left.

To our American cousins I wish,
HAPPY THANKSGIVING!

FRIDAY — NOVEMBER 23

MY good friend Doris Wimple says that to keep your children from listening in on your conversations, you should talk to them. As they grow up they will better communicate with their parents and Doris's own children are fine young people, and each one living proof of her point of view.

SATURDAY — NOVEMBER 24

QUEEN Mary, a friend was telling me recently, never drank liquor, never used a telephone or flew in a plane, and was never late for an appointment. Yet, even by contemporary standards, she led a full and active life. She lived long enough to see her granddaughter Elizabeth become Queen of England.

Perhaps I am being overly sentimental, but I still admire the old Queen and her virtues.

SUNDAY — NOVEMBER 25

WISDOM strengtheneth the wise more than ten mighty men which are in the city. For there is not a just man upon earth, that doeth good, and sinneth not.

MONDAY — NOVEMBER 26

SO long as suffering appears grievous to thee and thou seekest to fly from it, so long will it be ill with thee and the tribulation from which thou fliest will everywhere follow thee.

— *Thomas à Kempis*

TUESDAY — NOVEMBER 27

YOUNG children have such a lovely way of mangling things they do not fully understand. Last evening, while listening to my great-granddaughter's prayers, I heard this delightful invocation, "Give us this day our jelly bread . . . " It's just possible, of course, that Susan really meant it.

WEDNESDAY — NOVEMBER 28

WITH things so turbulent in our country these days, I have often wondered why people of good standing in the community are so unwilling to run for public office. And the answer, I am afraid, is quite simple. There is far too much unfair criticism of our public servants and too little praise for a job well done.

THURSDAY — NOVEMBER 29

INFLATION is when dollars-to-doughnuts becomes an even bet. Maybe I shouldn't be quite so flippant about our troubles, but before long doughnuts may indeed cost a dollar apiece.

FRIDAY — NOVEMBER 30

HERE's some thought about control which might be helpful as we enter the last month of the year.

> *You cannot control the length of your life, but you can control its width and depth.*

> *You cannot control the weather, but you can control the moral atmosphere which surrounds you.*

> *You cannot control the distance that your head shall be above ground, but you can control the height of the contents of your head.*

> *Why do we worry about things we cannot control? Why don't we get busy and control the things that depend on us?*

DECEMBER

SATURDAY — DECEMBER 1

"A green winter makes a fat churchyard." I can remember my grandmother saying so during a particularly mild winter, many years ago. I wonder if that marvelously shrewd lady ever realized that the old adage simply was not true. She probably did; she had a keen sense for practical medicine and irony.

SUNDAY — DECEMBER 2

A wrathful man stirreth up strife: but he that is slow to anger appeaseth strife.

MONDAY — DECEMBER 3

"THE younger generation isn't so bad; they just have more critics than models."

I wish I had been clever enough to think of that, but it was Rafe Josephs, the principal of a local school who deserves the credit.

TUESDAY — DECEMBER 4

IN September, Phyllis's friend Christie gave up her teaching job here in the city and moved to Rainy River, in northern Ontario. She came to see us the other day and I asked her why she had left a glamorous, lucrative position.

"Not enough pay," she said.

"But you were earning twice as much in Toronto!"

Christie smiled. "That's not what I meant, Mrs. McCann. In Rainy River I am doing something I love and really enjoy. In Toronto it was only the money, and that wasn't really enough."

I think she made the right choice. We must love what we do, for if we don't no amount of money can bring us happiness.

WEDNESDAY — DECEMBER 5

MRS. Findlay is an awfully wise woman who has had far more experience of life than many others. She claims that living is an art, more important, in fact, than music or painting or sculpture. "Trouble is," she was chuckling the other afternoon, "too few people learn to practice it successfully."

THURSDAY — DECEMBER 6

ANOTHER postcard from Edith, this time from Kicking Horse Pass. She claims to have passed a truck on the highway with this message in the rear window: "This truck has been in eight accidents and ain't lost any." Edith added that she kept a very safe distance from that truck. So would I.

FRIDAY — DECEMBER 7

MAN is the only animal that blushes. Or needs to.

— *Mark Twain*

SATURDAY — DECEMBER 8

HELEN Keller, that remarkable American lady, came to mind after talking with Harry Bellow, who's badly crippled with arthritis, especially now in the winter weather.

Miss Keller used to confess that she looked forward to the world here after "when all physical limitations will drop from me like shackles and I can engage joyously in greater service than I have yet known." Harry should take comfort in that.

SUNDAY — DECEMBER 9

AND he changeth the times and the seasons;
he removeth kings and setteth up kings;
he giveth wisdom unto the wise and knowledge to them that know understanding;

He revealeth deep and secret things: he knoweth what is in the darkness, and the light dwelleth with him.

MONDAY — DECEMBER 10

OUR first snowfall. It seems to come earlier than ever now. The weather experts have been telling us that the climate is changing: colder winters and cooler summers. But all their jargon doesn't detract from the peace and quiet that envelop the house tonight. Everything looks so clean and fresh and lovely. In a few days, of course, the snow will turn gray and mushy, and next March we'll all wish we had never seen it.

TUESDAY — DECEMBER 11

ON the way to the hairdresser's I passed this sign outside a small church: "This is a CH—ch. What's missing?" I had a pleasant chuckle: "You are."

WEDNESDAY — DECEMBER 12

MY friend's daughter found a large unfamiliar parcel all wrapped up in foil in her freezer. Being curious, she opened it and found four dozen snowballs. Her enquiries brought forth no explanations, so she decided to throw them out. Suddenly there was a dreadful wail from nine-year-old Kevin: "Oh, Mummy, please don't throw them out. I'll make a fortune next August selling real snowballs."

I was so delighted with the story, I forgot to ask Ruth if she kept them.

THURSDAY — DECEMBER 13

LEARNING is like rowing upstream: not to advance is to drop back.

— *Chinese proverb*

FRIDAY — DECEMBER 14

MY neighbor's six-year-old daughter was taken to the hospital to see her new baby brother.

"What do you think of him?" I asked. Disappointed that he was not a sister she stammered, "He's, he's, just my favorite shade of red."

SATURDAY — DECEMBER 15

IT'S not what you say that's important between friends; it's never needing to say it
—that's what counts.

SUNDAY — DECEMBER 16

THE Lord is my shepherd; I shall not want.
He maketh me to lie down in green pas-
tures; he leadeth me beside the still waters.

He restoreth my soul: he leadeth me in the
paths of righteousness for his name's sake.

Yea, though I walk through the valley of the
shadow of death, I will fear no evil; for though
art with me; thy rod and thy staff they comfort
me.

MONDAY — DECEMBER 17

YOUNG Timothy came home from school
yesterday with a black eye. His mother
angrily asked if he'd been in another fight.

"Just keeping a little guy from being beat up
by a bigger boy."

His mother's anger disappeared. "That was
brave of you, dear. Who was the little boy?"

"Me, Mommy."

TUESDAY — DECEMBER 18

THE play of animals is just their way of uttering the glory of God.

— *Novalis*

WEDNESDAY — DECEMBER 19

POOR Muriel, in the rush of last-minute Christmas shopping she bought a box of twenty-five identical greeting cards. Not bothering to read the verse, she hastily signed and addressed all but one. Yesterday, after all the cards had been mailed, she came across the remaining one and looked at the message. To her horror she read: "This is just a note to say / A little gift is on its way."

THURSDAY — DECEMBER 20

WE can all so easily be rich, not rich in material things but rich in things of the spirit. All we need to do is think of Christmas and its happiness: children, food, gifts, a loving family and friends. Or we can reach further back into our memories to love and happy times. No, not one of us need ever fear poverty.

FRIDAY — DECEMBER 21

"LET me not neglect any kindness, for I shall not pass this way again."

So often have I remembered those wise words these past days. They are a useful reminder to do good.

SATURDAY — DECEMBER 22

MANY of the family have begun to arrive: daughters, sons-in-law, grandchildren, even a few great-grandchildren.

Like so many other families, we are all busy preparing for the feast of Christmas. The best part, perhaps, is now when all my family are with me.

SUNDAY — DECEMBER 23

AND when Elizabeth heard the greeting of Mary, the babe leaped in her womb; and Elizabeth was filled with the Holy Spirit and she exclaimed with a loud cry, "Blessed are you among women, and blessed is the fruit of your womb."

MONDAY — DECEMBER 24

YEARS ago, at a little village in New Brunswick, I remember seeing the most extraordinary Christmas tree, one that combined the true spirit of giving with a sense of humor.

The tree was decorated with lobster buoys and fishing nets and tackle. Its trunk was hidden away by neatly stacked lobster pots.

I wonder if the villages still celebrate Christmas in their own way, or have they, like so many others, given in to artificial trees?

TUESDAY — DECEMBER 25

LORD, now lettest thou thy servant depart in peace, according to thy word:

For mine eyes have seen thy salvation,

Which thou hast prepared before the face of all people;

A light to lighten the Gentiles, and the glory of thy people Israel.

With so many members of my family here, the day has been a joyous and loving one. At such times I am convinced that the world is truly good and kind.

CHRISTMAS BLESSING, EVERYONE.

WEDNESDAY — DECEMBER 26

THIS morning many of the stores are open again for after-Christmas sales. I have never truly understood why, the day after Christmas, anyone would want to rush out again to do more shopping. It seems to me that this is the one week of the year when we should be visiting with family and friends.

THURSDAY — DECEMBER 27

AUNT May, one of our Christmas guests, explained to us why her personal possessions have become so important to her in her old age.

"It's not that I'm materialistic, Lord knows I've never hankered after things for their own sake. But it's the associations these things have for me—they've come to symbolize the loveliest experiences of my life. Do you understand?"

Of course we do.

FRIDAY — DECEMBER 28

HUMAN love and the delights of friendship, out of which are built the memories that endure, are also to be treasured up as hints of what shall be in the hereafter.

— *Bede Jarrett*

SATURDAY — DECEMBER 29

MY daughter loves to tell this story about old Mr. Birtwhistle, who retired from farming many years ago.

Apparently he ran into a young businessman one day and, of course, that old chestnut came up in discussion. Which is better—life in the city or life in the country?

The businessman, as might be expected, forthrightly presented his views, and said he preferred living in the city for many reasons.

And then Mr. Birtwhistle, with that gravelly voice and that wicked chuckle we all knew so well, said: "Young man, I figure it this way. That city of yours shouts about the works of man. But the country—well, to a lot of folks like us the country whispers about the works of God."

SUNDAY — DECEMBER 30

NOW ye have consecrated yourselves unto the Lord, come near and bring sacrifices and thank offerings unto the house of the Lord.

MONDAY — DECEMBER 31

ON the last day of the year, I like to think about my favorite lines from Ecclesiastes and present them to you.

To every thing there is a season, and a time to every purpose under the heaven:

A time to be born, and a time to die; a time to plant, and a time to pluck up that which is planted;

A time to kill, and a time to heal; a time to break down, and a time to build up;

A time to weep, and a time to laugh; a time to mourn, and a time to dance;

A time to cast away stones, and a time to gather stones together; a time to embrace, and a time to refrain from embracing;

A time to get, and a time to lose; a time to keep, and a time to cast away;

A time to rend, and a time to sew; a time to keep silence, and a time to speak;

A time to love, and a time to hate; a time of war, and a time of peace.

**A HAPPY, HEALTHY AND
PEACEFUL NEW YEAR!**

PICTURE CREDITS